Rochelle Lang

Disclaimer

She Moves Mountains is a ministry focused on prayer, spiritual growth, and fostering a deeper, more intimate relationship with the Lord. Our purpose is to guide individuals in discovering and understanding their identity through connection with the Creator's heart.

Please note that *She Moves Mountains* is not a mental health or counseling ministry. We do not provide professional mental health services, therapy, or counseling. The content shared through our book, classes, and other resources is intended to support your spiritual journey and relationship with God.

If you are experiencing mental health challenges or require professional counseling, we strongly encourage you to seek help from a licensed mental health professional or counselor. The practices and teachings provided in this ministry are complementary to, but not a substitute for, professional mental health care.

By participating in this ministry, you acknowledge that *She Moves Mountains* is not responsible for any decisions or actions you take based on the spiritual guidance provided. Your spiritual growth and well-being are deeply important to us, and we are committed to supporting you in your walk with the Lord, within the scope of our ministry's purpose.

For additional information,

Visit our website:

www.shemovesmountains.live

Dedication

To my amazing children, Tyler, Jonah, and Madeline, and to my wonderful children by heart, Camille, Kenzie, and Jessica. Your strength, love, and resilience inspire me every day.

To my incredible grandchildren, who represent our new legacy and bring hope and healing to our tribe: thank you for your laughter and light. You are the future, and it's a joy to watch you grow.

To the deep friendships that inspired me along the way, encouraging me to keep going and to be authentic with myself and with this project. Your unwavering support and belief in me have been invaluable.

This work is for all of you, with all my love and gratitude.

FOREWORD

Everyone has heart wounds that need healing. Rochelle shares her story of how Jesus healed the broken pieces in her heart. She wants others to know that this kind of healing prayer is available and is effective.

She also lets you know that healing takes time, and that healing comes in layers. We wish healing would be instant, but the Bible says, "We have the prophetic word made more sure, to which you do well to pay attention as to a lamp shining in a dark place, **until the day dawns and the morning star arises in your hearts**. (2 Pet. 1:19)

I have found this verse to be true in my own life. Having been a Christian for 57 years, I find that every year the **light gets brighter**. I see things more clearly. I walk in greater obedience. I discover I can have greater love, joy, peace, and health.

Yes, greater health is one wonderful benefit of greater Kingdom emotions. The Kingdom is joy and peace (Rom. 14:17) and the fruit of the Spirit includes love (Gal. 5:22). So, expect love, joy, and peace to increase within you as you read this book. As you listen to Rochelle share her healing, expectation grows. Faith grows. Hope grows and hope brings revelation, insight, and healing.

Rochelle covers the four keys to hearing God's voice, which are: Becoming still, seeing Jesus with you, recognizing His voice as flowing thoughts, and journaling out this flow of thoughts and pictures.

The day I discovered these four keys for myself and used them as a bundle was the day my Christian life changed from law to grace. I had been a Christian for ten years and hungered to hear His voice. Finally, the breakthrough came one morning as God awakened me and said, "Get up! I'm going to teach you to hear My voice."

That morning, He taught me these four keys and I spent the entire day journaling out the two-way dialogue I was having with Him. See my story here: www.CWGministries.org/4keys.

I write and teach from a left-brain perspective, while Rochelle shares her story from a right-brain perspective. Both are valuable. Both have a place. Rochelle agrees that it is the voice of the Wonderful Counselor that heals our hearts as we receive and act on His wonderful counsel.

I pray this book inspires you to reach out to God, and by hearing His voice and seeing His vision, you receive His wonderful counsel. NOTHING in life compares to this.

It is also wise to reach out to prayer counselors who offer specialized prayer ministry that heals heart wounds and through them to receive your healing. I have watched Jesus heal layer after layer of wounds in my own heart as I have experienced inner healing and deliverance, along with other prayers such as breaking generational curses, severing ungodly soul ties, replacing ungodly beliefs and inner vows with godly beliefs and godly purposes, and breaking off word curses. Walking in freedom is a wonderful gift and it is available to all who earnestly pursue God with a passion to be whole and to be set free.

Our prayer is that God moves mountains in your heart, granting you a healed heart, and that you become a mountain mover with Christ.

Dr. Mark Virkler

Founder and President – Communion With God Ministries & Christian Leadership University

Table of Contents

How to Use This Book

Welcome to *She Moves Mountains*, a journey designed to deepen your relationship with God and foster meaningful connections with others. This book is a guide to experiencing personal healing and growth through community and shared faith.

1. Engage: Each chapter is crafted to lead you through a process of reflection, prayer, and action. Take your time with each section, allowing the teachings to resonate and inspire transformation.

2. Participate in Group Discussions: Use this book as a tool for group discussions. Gather with other women to share insights, experiences, and encouragement.

3. Apply the Lessons: The practical steps outlined in this book, along with the workbook, are designed to be implemented in your daily life. As you practice these principles, you will see growth in your relationships with God, family, friends, and community.

4. Reflect and Journal: Reflecting on your experiences and recording your thoughts will help solidify your learning and highlight areas of personal growth.

How This Book Affects Our Lives

This book will teach us how to walk through healing. We will learn to take time to listen to each other, understanding that who we and our stories are both important to the heart of God. Women play a pivotal role in transforming families, communities, and beyond. By nurturing and guiding those around them, women have the power to inspire change and healing.

This book encourages you to embrace this influence by fostering a supportive network of women who are committed to growth and authenticity.

1. Building Authentic Relationships: As you journey through this book, you will build deeper relationships with other women, creating a community where you can be genuine and vulnerable. This authenticity is key to personal healing and to helping others heal.

2. Empowering Each Other: By sharing your stories and listening to others, you will experience the power of collective wisdom and encouragement. This book encourages you to support one another, recognizing that together, we can achieve more.

3. Experiencing Transformation: Through engaging with the teachings in this book, you will invite God's presence into your life, experiencing His kindness and compassion. This relationship with God will empower you to bring about transformation in your own life and the lives of others.

At, *She Moves Mountains*, we believe that healing ourselves equips us to heal others. By using this book, you will embark on a journey of personal growth that extends beyond yourself, impacting your family, community, and even the world.

Rochelle Lang

Founder *She Moves Mountains*

HE STILL MOVES

Keep creating in me a clean heart. Fill me with pure thoughts and holy desires, ready to please you. May you never reject me! May you never take from me your sacred Spirit! Let my passion for life be restored, tasting joy in every breakthrough you bring to me. Hold me close to you with a willing spirit that obeys whatever you say."
Psalms 51:10-12 TPT

Chapter One: He Still Moves

In a world marked by brokenness and confusion, the journey to healing and wholeness begins at the cross. This chapter explores the profound transformation that occurs when we turn to God, embrace His unchanging character, and walk the path of repentance and forgiveness. Through personal stories and biblical insights, we uncover the relentless love of God, the power of Jesus' sacrifice, and the hope that extends from our own lives to the nations. As we delve into the depths of His grace, we discover the unquenchable thirst that only Jesus can satisfy, bringing freedom and restoration to a weary world.

Just like Esther, who emerged from her orphanhood into her regal call and purpose in destiny, you too are being called to something significant for the current season in which we live—such a time as this. We play a critical role in bringing about the transformation of our world from a heavenly perspective to the earthly reality. It is intended for us to live out the prayer Jesus gave:

Our Father in heaven, hallowed be your name. Your kingdom come, your will be done, on earth as it is in heaven.[1] Just as Esther was diligently prepared for her battle, we too, need to be battle-ready: healed, whole, and fully prepared to engage in the role God has designed for us in our time. It's not just for us, beautiful women. It's for our people. It's for our region. It's for our nation and the nations spanning the earth.

Welcome to *She Moves Mountains*. It is the pathway of preparation we will travel together. This venture will require authenticity; it will require taking chances, and risking being vulnerable. In doing so, you will be granted a powerful opportunity for the breakthrough, healing, and restoration needed to be an integral part of bringing Heaven to Earth. I am grateful you have accepted the invitation—and the challenge—to embark on this journey with us. You were strategically born for such a time as this.[2]

Our pathway begins when the earth was without form and void, and darkness was over the face of the deep. Then Adonai, which means LORD, spoke everything into existence: On the first day, He created light, separating it from darkness, calling the light 'Day' and the darkness 'Night.'[3] On the second day, He formed the expanse, separating the waters from the waters, and called the expanse 'Heaven.'[4] On the third day, He gathered the waters under the heavens into one place, letting dry land appear, and brought forth vegetation, plants yielding seed, and fruit trees bearing fruit according to their kinds.[5] He created lights in the expanse of the heavens to separate day from night and to mark seasons.[6] On the fifth day, He filled the waters with living creatures and let birds fly above the earth.[7] On the sixth day, He brought forth living creatures of various kinds and made man in His own image, giving them dominion over all creatures.[8] God created man in His own image, in the image of God he created him; male and female he created them. And God blessed them. And God said to them, "Be fruitful and multiply and fill the earth and subdue it."[9]

In the Garden of Eden, Adam and Eve were not just caretakers of creation but were deeply loved and cherished by God, meeting face to face with their Creator. From the beginning, Adonai visited them in the garden, walking with them in the cool of the day. Imagine walking with the Lord in a world where all the animals were like pets, the lamb lying down with the lion—a vision of rest and safety. God's profound love for them invited them into intimate communion and community with Him. We loved because He loved us so well, drawing us into His embrace. Yet, in this paradise, there was one tree from which Adonai commanded them not to eat: the tree of the knowledge of good and evil, for eating from it would lead to death.[10] A serpent, the adversary, convinced Adam and Eve that God was withholding something from them, leading Eve to see the tree as good for food, a delight to the eyes, and desirable for gaining wisdom.[11] She took its fruit, ate it, and gave some to her husband, who also ate. Upon eating, Adam and Eve realized their nakedness, hid, and covered themselves with fig leaves.[12] This is a stark illustration of how, then, and today, shame can lead us to hide or cover ourselves with our own fig leaves. When God asked, "Where are you?" He sought Adam and Eve to speak with them, but sin had created a separation.[13] In the aftermath, Adam blamed Eve, Eve blamed the serpent, and curses were pronounced on the serpent, Eve, and Adam.[14]

This being so, the Lord said, "Fig leaves will simply not do." And He sacrificed the first animal to cover their nakedness. Thus, the first sacrifice occurred, foreshadowing the ultimate sacrifice that was to come. Despite this, one undeniable truth remained: death and sin had entered mankind. A sacrifice was necessary—yet it would not fully satisfy.

As the journey continues, Adam and Eve are told to be fruitful and multiply, leading to the birth of Cain and Abel. The need for sacrifices remained, a perpetual act to seek Adonai's forgiveness and to make atonement for the sin of man.

Cain brought his offering from the fruits of the ground, but Adonai, upon examining his heart, found it insufficient. Abel, in contrast, brought the firstlings of his flock, the best of his lambs, and their fat portions, just as Adonai had instructed. Abel had obeyed with a pure heart. Thus, Adonai accepted Abel's offering but rejected that of Cain. This stirred up discontentment in Cain's heart. In His grace and mercy, Adonai spoke to Cain, encouraging him to do right and warning of sin personified, lurking at the door. Yet Cain, in his stubbornness and in contempt of Adonai, chose his own path. He wretchedly sacrificed the blood of his own brother. How often have we been placed on the altar as a sacrifice as a result of someone else's choices? Or how frequently have we sacrificed others for our own defense, for the concealment of our own sin, or because of shame? All of these actions must ultimately be brought to the altar of repentance.

At this point in the journey, I'll intersect our path with that of my own. I came to believe in Jesus at four years old when I encountered Him through a dream. In that moment, I longed to be with Him, knowing He was real. I remember picking up my blankey and doll and telling Jesus, "OK, I'm ready to go." The experience felt profoundly real. Even at that young age, I felt a deep need for a Savior and saw no other way out. I didn't want to continue living as I was. It's a big decision for a little four-year-old to wish she had never been born or to seek an escape from the chaos surrounding her. By the time I was four, I had already experienced abuse.

One summer day while I was playing in my backyard alone, I was coaxed out of the yard with a piece of candy, only to be thrown into a tent where a group of boys began to force themselves on me. If it hadn't been for the voice in the background saying, "She's a live one, let's let her go," I'm not sure what would have happened. Thankfully, they let me go. I was so young and lost. After somehow finding my way home, I told my mother what had happened. Instead of comfort, I was starkly reprimanded for leaving the yard and sent to my room. Unbeknownst to me at the time, my mother's reaction was triggered by her own traumatic experience of being assaulted at four years old. It was a generational curse coming down the line, filled with fear and anger.

In my tiny heart, I made some strong decisions that day. I felt all alone in the world, with no one to comfort me. I vowed to protect myself by closing off my heart, convinced that I couldn't trust anyone. Each judgment and vow I had made throughout my life laid another brick in front of the door to my heart. These bricks, built from many stories of abuse, reinforced what my heart had decided: "You can't trust anyone," and "You're in it alone and must take care of yourself." With each brick, the space around me felt smaller and colder. Soon, I found myself writing words about who I believed I was on the walls of that dark place: "unloved," "unwanted," "unworthy." These words starkly echoed the strongholds of lies I believed: "I am not enough," and "I am too much."

For years, I dealt with that trauma alone, unaware that Jesus had been with me all along. The realization came gradually, like the first light of dawn gently breaking through the darkness. I didn't realize that a part of my heart was held captive to that memory, but He promised He would guide me to freedom. He gently led me on this journey, showing me what healing felt like and revealing how deeply He cared for me. Jesus didn't tear down the wall abruptly. Instead, we gently removed each brick, one by one, receiving them with compassion. As He opened the space, light and warmth began to fill the room, inviting me to step out of my self-imposed prison. With the help of those who loved me and prayed with me, I was able to be set fee. They guided me towards an encounter with Jesus through the Holy Spirit, showing me the way to true freedom and healing.

In that dream at four years old, Jesus found me and let me know He was real. From that day on, I believed there was one I could learn to trust. I didn't fully grasp it then—I was still young—but He came to help me know He was real and present, even in the chaos. That dream encounter at four years old is something I will never forget; it solidified in me the reality of Jesus as my Savior.

For me, the real quest for freedom started in my early 20s as I broke away from a past marred by dysfunction and abuse. I had the upbringing—a

Bible college education, and a life in the church since I was little. But something heavy lingered. Despite fitting the "good girl" image in my church community, I carried a lot of pain. When I tried to share, I found others were just as hurt. Not sure who to turn to, I kept my struggles to myself. I remember praying in my small apartment, telling God I didn't want to know Him if He was anything like my mother's unpredictable and harsh version. I opened my heart to a different, more loving God, if He was out there, and to my surprise, that's when healing began. I was able to start the journey up the mountain to break free from the judgments I had made toward others, myself, and God in response to the pain.

I was challenged to ask the questions: What did my heart come to believe in the pain? How did I choose to protect my heart? He gently came to my rescue, helping me turn away from wrong beliefs and embrace His words over me—that I was loved and that He had always been there. He understood my pain, but He wouldn't let me stay there. He would rescue me. I needed a Savior, and it was God's grace that encountered me, confirming His reality.

After that prayer, it wasn't long before I was offered a job as a counselor at a juvenile detention center in a small town in Idaho. I quickly became involved in a small church where the people introduced me to the teachings of John and Paula Sandford, pioneers in the inner healing and emotional healing movement. I eagerly absorbed their lectures, keen to apply their principles to my own life. My friends and I supported each other's growth, challenging one another to confront and change our unhealthy habits. Despite feelings of jealousy and rejection, I faced the truth about my behavior and faulty belief systems thanks to their kindness and honest conversations within a safe community. Many times, I wanted to run because a trauma brain often perceives safety as a threat. However,

I stayed because the people loved me in the midst of my pain. They stayed up nights to pray for me and became mothers and fathers in my life.

This led me to prayer ministry with someone seasoned in listening to the Holy Spirit and prayer—not just a counselor. I embraced both the support and challenges it brought. Inner healing often brings about deliverance from spirits that have been assigned to keep you stuck in old, dangerous thought patterns. Through this process, I experienced profound personal freedom and transformation.

As I underwent my own deliverance, I became aware of a larger movement at play. We were a part of a deliverance movement, a profound and intense time that I believe is on the horizon again. This movement is not just about individual healing, but about a collective awakening and freedom for many. It's difficult to predict how it will manifest this time, but I anticipate it will be uniquely different from the past. During my journey, I sought God's guidance out of my despair and hopelessness and found freedom in His presence through the love and support of the church community and family. Now, I see this same potential for freedom and transformation on a national scale.

Reflecting on those days, I remember sitting across from my prayer minister. She asked me who my God was. I described a scenario of an "angry sinner in the hands of an angry God." I told her how I saw myself as a good girl, but I could never be good enough. I was constantly trying, but He was always finding my faults and making me out to be worse than I was. Those very questions helped me discover that I didn't have the right God on the throne of my life. That is why it's so important that we ask each other the questions that get to the heart! This is where we discover the truth that will set us free.

The prayer minister then asked me, "Would you like to renounce the god who has been sitting on the throne?" By God's grace, I was given a vision and I finally saw it clearly—the most hideous god sat on my throne. I responded, "Yes. I don't know how he got there, but I am ready to renounce that god. When I was young, I chose to believe in Him but lived my life only knowing of Him." Now there was an invitation to have Him live in me, leading my life and teaching me His ways. It would mean changing from a self-centered faith to a God-centered one.

I repented of my sins that very day and began the journey toward what I later coined as the well-worn pathway of the cross. I invited Jesus to be the LORD of my life. I wanted His way and His desire for me. As I did, I experienced the most incredible moments of renewal and refreshing in His presence. That day, I understood what it felt like to be clean for the very first time; to be forgiven at long last. As though I had known of Him and believed in Him, I had not made Him Lord of my life. It wouldn't be long, only six or seven weeks later, that I would start to have flashbacks of the abuse—the memories of the pain and the trauma I had suffered as a child had finally seeped to the forefront of my soul.[15] I had to walk through these memories piece by piece; a little here, a little there. And then I would find respite and rest.[16]

By the time I was 39 years old, I had worked through much with my church leaders, pastors, and friends. However, there were deeper issues that I couldn't resolve without professional help. Despite continually finding small measures of freedom, I still struggled with feelings of inadequacy, abandonment, and not being good enough. Desperate for greater healing, I found myself at the doorstep of a healing ministry. I recognized my profound need for healing in my heart. My prayer minister began to guide me through deeper healing, where I had to be honest and vulnerable about my stories (James 5:16)[17]. It was in that place of honesty and vulnerability that God, Adonai, met me. In the course of my journey, I had so often found myself back on that throne, attempting to take control of my life. It is only through the beautiful grace of God that we are forgiven and can truly find the healing and peace we seek.

The pathway to the cross is well-worn because we walk it many times, each journey deepening our healing and understanding. As we become more familiar with this route, we come to cherish the incredible gifts it brings: forgiveness, the death of our sins in Jesus Christ, and the joy of living in His resurrection. This path ushers us into a new life, where the blood of Jesus meets all requirements to cover not only our personal sins but also those of all mankind.[18] In His name, Yeshua, Jesus, every requirement is met, and the enemy must flee.[19] His name breaks away all that hinders our lives, aligning us with God's plan for our good.[20]

As we embark on this journey of learning about God and His character, I assure you, as the Bible says, that He is faithful from beginning to end. His character remains consistent; His ways are unchanging. I am learning to trust Him over and over again as things present themselves, especially when I feel like there is nothing good or right within me—feeling completely out of alignment with God. But God remains faithful, true to His character, inviting us into His presence and offering His perfect pathway to salvation.

I cherish the fact that He declares the way to the Father—the only path— is through the Son. He extends an invitation for us to repent of our sins, to acknowledge our own faults, addictions, perversions, jealousy, envy, lust, and self-seeking desires. He calls us to be honest about these, to admit we need Him to forgive us and lead us, not to dwell in shame, but to accept the guilt, knowing that it is swiftly forgiven at the cross because of the blood of Jesus that satisfies all requirements. This journey of repentance and forgiveness stretches far beyond our personal lives—to those around us, our regions, our nation, and even to the nations. When Abel's blood cried out from the ground in Genesis 4:10, God confronted Cain, declaring, "Cain, your brother's blood demands justice, and I am compelled to act." Across our land, blood has been shed from tribe to tribe, nation to nation, person to person, fueling a cycle of insatiable destruction. This leads to escalating abortion and suicide, among other atrocities. Yet through the power of the cross, the debt can be resolved—in us and then through us. Our thirst, and their thirst, can only be quenched by Jesus.

God is compelled to act justly in response to the bloodshed on our nation's soil, as He embodies Justice itself. The adversary tries to exploit this, but there's a powerful counterforce: the blood of Jesus, fulfilling all requirements and providing a redemptive solution.[21] This blood meets the adversary's demand for justice, freeing us and providing justification as if we had never sinned.[22] Jesus bore our sins on the cross. [23] Approaching the cross through His plan leads to freedom. Today, I invite you to journey along the well-trodden path to the cross, where we can find true freedom. The Bible mentions a narrow road that few find.[24] Isn't it striking that the world has discovered so many other paths to reach God? We've become community members, we love our groups and our people, but God calls us to something much richer and deeper. This path is unfathomable, transformative, and sets us apart. He's inviting us to come to the cross, to kneel, bend our knee, and admit that it's only about Jesus.[25]

Today, I invite us to come together in prayer once again. If we've been hiding behind masks or following our own paths, if we've acknowledged Him as our Savior but not as the Lord of our lives, and then as our Healer, there is no better time than now to embark on this transformative journey. Let's approach Him in the manner in which He calls us to. Let's pray, "God, I repent," and take a moment to acknowledge the things we are aware of even now. The Lord will gently lead us, step by step, through our need for repentance and forgiveness on this journey. We begin today at the cross. This is where the true path starts. Before we can face giants, before we can climb the mountain and move mountains, our faith must be securely anchored. We must approach Him in His way.

Take some time to write in your journal.
1. *What does salvation mean to you personally?*
2. *Reflect on a moment when you felt the Lord moving in your life. How did it change you?*
3. *Have you invited Jesus to be Lord over different areas of your life? Tell your story.*

Prayer
Heavenly Father,
I repent for trying to be the master of my own life. I change my mind about who I want to be in charge of my life. I turn from my useless and unproductive thoughts that say I am the center of my universe and I choose instead to believe in the living God who created everything, including me.[26] I have lived without purpose, but now I will live to hear and obey You, God.[27]
I confess with my lips that Jesus is Lord, and I believe in my heart that God raised Him from the dead. I believe that God so loved the world He sent His only Son, Jesus, to shed His blood to wash away the barrier of sin.[28] I receive You, Jesus, as MY Lord and Savior.[29] I welcome You, Holy Spirit, into my life to rescue and empower me and to restore me to intimacy with my heavenly Father.[30] In Jesus' name, I pray. Amen.

HIS PRESENCE

Because I set you, Yahweh, always close to me,
my confidence will never be weakened,
for I experience your wraparound presence every moment.

Psalms 16:8 TPT

Chapter Two – His Wrap Around Presence

We stand at the brink of a momentous and transformative decade. The coming radical shift will potentially create moments of uncertainty—yet in it and through it, God will reveal Himself and deliver His salvation, leading His people back to Him.

God can, like no other, rouse a generation bound in the depths of darkness and weighed down by poverty of spirit. Through the outpouring of the Holy Spirit, He intends to ignite among this generation a season of revival, restoration, and reformation never seen before. It is His Presence that transforms us from the inside out, deepening our relationship with God and teaching us to stand strong, walk in His ways, and love—others and ourselves.

In this chapter, we will be introduced to the profound presence of Holy Spirit. Without knowing Him, navigating through life, walking in the fullness of our purpose, or restoring the places wounded by life's challenges is impossible.

Holy Spirit is a precious gift from the Father, who instructed the Son to send Him to us. The Father had this in mind when He invited Jesus to sit at His right hand, promising to put Jesus' enemies under His feet.[1] Yet, He did not leave us alone, forgotten, abandoned, or orphaned. Instead, He wanted us to have everything we needed to successfully navigate this life.

His thoughts and dreams for us, like a good father's dreams for his children or a creator's intentions for the created, are for us to live in the fullness of His love and goodness, walking in the full color of our purpose. To walk in

His design, we must have both Jesus as Lord of our lives, and a deep, personal relationship with Holy Spirit.

In the last days, Jesus promised, "I will pour out my Spirit on all flesh, and your sons and your daughters shall prophesy, and your young men shall see visions, and your old men shall dream dreams; even on my male servants and female servants in those days I will pour out my Spirit, and they shall prophesy."[2]

When I began my healing journey, I was so desperate for freedom that I wanted to dive straight into fixing my wounds and overcoming my traumas. However, Holy Spirit guided me down a different path—one that involved studying the names of God. This guidance came in the form of cassettes from a Bible teacher, Kay Arthur, titled "Lord, I Want to Know You," a study of the names of God. These cassettes arrived at my door once a month; I would listen to them over and over, studying each name of God until I truly began to believe in His character.

Initially, I found this approach frustrating. I thought I already knew God and just wanted to get healed as quickly as possible. But in reality, I didn't truly know Him. During this time of growth, I learned the importance of Holy Spirit. He is with us always, no matter where we go. Yet, it's easy to be unaware of this presence, especially when overwhelmed by pain and seeking immediate solutions. When existing in a heightened state of trauma, there's an urgency to fix everything right away. We often want to skip straight to the healing without laying the proper foundation of true salvation and understanding Holy Spirit's guidance in our lives. But without that foundation, we have nothing to anchor us to truth during the healing process.

During this period of healing, I would experience quick, fleeting flashbacks, like a lamp with a short circuit. As soon as the wires connected for a brief moment, the light would reveal the memory of the pain and sorrow of what had happened to me. In an instant, I would be filled with the fear of that experience and break down as though my life was unraveling before me. No one could console me. However, if they were able to sit with me in quietness, comfort, and stay present, I had an easier time coming back to a settled space. After the shock, terror, and fear subsided, I would be able to tell bits of the story. It would be awkward at first because I didn't know how to recount a story, I was barely becoming familiar with again. It would emerge at random times, and I'd feel so embarrassed because I didn't know how to really share. It was a part of my early childhood, so it was coming from the heart of a child trying to explain the dysfunction of a family and the pain of abuse through a child's eyes.

In those days, I didn't fully grasp the depth of who Jesus was—but I knew He was real. That year of learning about His character set a firm foundation for me to begin trusting Him. He was helping and guiding me through Holy Spirit to touch into the pain, and then He would lead me to a place of rest so I could heal. Jesus, through Holy Spirit, never overwhelmed me; He helped me process it. The enemy tries to overload our circuits, so we won't look at the pain and walk through it. This is why it's so important to have a solid foundation of who Jesus is, who Father God is, and who Holy Spirit is in our lives. Jesus does not want to re-traumatize us or remind us of our pain and sorrow. He only wants us to go deep enough to close the doors to the enemy by coming out of the agreements we have made with our own judgments of the situation, our vows and false refuges of our solutions independent of Him, and the lies we have written on the walls of our hearts. Jesus wants to wash those words away and replace them with who He says we are. I love the verse that says, "For I know the plans I have for you, declares the Lord, plans for welfare and not for evil, to give you a future and a hope."[3]

Studying the names of God through those times taught me about His character and His timeless nature. This timelessness contrasts sharply with our reliance on time to heal our wounds. We often believe that if we just endure long enough, time will heal all wounds. However, the timeless covenant of the blood of Jesus, not time, is what truly heals us. The quote that comes to mind is: "What is buried alive, stays alive."

Instead, we can learn to recognize the enemy of our souls and place our trust in God's unwavering faithfulness. By doing so, we align ourselves with the timeless truth that Jesus Christ is the same yesterday, today, and forever.[4]

Through this process, I came to understand that true healing comes from a deep relationship with God, anchored in the knowledge of His character and the guidance of Holy Spirit. This foundation is what sustains us through the challenges and pain we encounter, allowing us to experience the fullness of His healing power.

How do we become so confused in our understanding that we blame God for the difficulties in our lives, instead of recognizing the enemy's efforts to steal, kill, and destroy? We often overlook that God's principles and natural laws are constantly at work whether we believe in Him or not. When we disregard these principles—whether out of our own choosing, misunderstanding, or lack of knowledge—we face consequences. Yet, we wrongly attribute these consequences to God, when in reality, they stem from our own and others' choices. And it is through the blood of Jesus and the work of Holy Spirit in our lives that we are set free. That's why we need Holy Spirit—He constantly reveals to us the goodness of God, His character, who He is—and heals us because of it. If you know your Father, then you know who you are. You gain your identity from Him.

Holy Spirit reveals the Father to us, and then the Father reveals who we are. There's a misconception that it's all about God and none about us, but the truth is, God created us uniquely. He gave us different personalities, looks, and gifts. When we receive a compliment, we shouldn't say, "It's all God," but rather understand that He created us to uniquely reflect His image.

God thinks highly of His creation. He designed us to manifest Him in our unique ways. Instead of saying, "Less of me and more of God," what if we focused on thoughts such as these: "God, heal my pain. Let me know You. Teach me who You say I am. Help me walk in my true identity and become all I'm meant to be as one who carries Your glory and light." By knowing our identity in Him, we partner with Him in our daily lives.

This knowledge of the functioning of Holy Spirit is essential for us to know. Many people don't understand Him or were taught that He was only for those who came before us. But the truth is, we need Holy Spirit because Jesus said, "I am going to prepare a place for you, but I am sending you a Comforter, someone who will lead you into all truth." Sadly, in our religious traditions, we often ignore Holy Spirit, not comprehending that we won't find freedom by just pushing through or ignoring the issue.

Therefore, let's seek to understand and embrace Holy Spirit's role in our lives. Let's allow Him to lead us into all truth, helping us to recognize our true identity and purpose. This relationship with God brings freedom, healing, and a deeper understanding of who we are meant to be.

Pentecost - The Coming Wind of Holy Spirit

Without Holy Spirit, we cannot fulfill our purpose as God's people, as His sons and daughters. On the same day in history, known as Pentecost or *Shavuot* in Hebrew, we see a profound connection. In Acts chapter 2, Holy Spirit was given. What many often overlook is that on this same day, many years previously, God descended on Mount Sinai and delivered the Ten Commandments, marking it as the day of the giving of Instruction or *Torah* in Hebrew. Why do the Spirit of God and the Word of God converge on the same day? The significance is profound. Consider how God created the world: His Spirit hovered over the face of the deep, and God spoke, transforming chaos into order and darkness into light. Similarly, new creation comes about through God's Word, applied to our lives and empowered by the Spirit of God.

And we see this in the life of Peter. Peter was full of the Word, right? He had spent three and a half years studying at the feet of the Master Teacher Jesus. But at the death of Jesus, Peter winds up denying the Lord and locking himself in the upper room, scared to be seen. Then, seven weeks later, on Pentecost, he stands up in front of all the religious leaders and everyone in Jerusalem, preaching a fiery Pentecost message that leads thousands to believe. That's what happens when the Spirit of God comes upon us. When we're filled with the Word of God, it not only changes us and transforms us from the inside out but also makes a huge impact on the lives of those around us.

How can we integrate both the Word of God and the guidance of Holy Spirit into our daily lives? The Word of God is the weapon the Lord has given us. Jesus overcame the temptations of the enemy by quoting Scripture: "Man does not live by bread alone, but by every word that comes out of the mouth of God." Knowing God's Word is important because, going back to the Fall, the serpent persuaded Eve to doubt God's Word—"Did the Lord really say?" When we know the truth, it helps us overcome the lies. When we believe lies, we empower the liar and become captive to those lies. And in our trauma, we have believed some pretty amazing lies about ourselves and others that do not agree with what God says about who we are. When we can dismantle those lies with the truth, it sets us free. The greatest weapon is the truth, and with so much misinformation, lies, and falsehoods coming at us, we must know the unchangeable, unshakable truth to combat them, to be transformed, and to have the wisdom to walk out God's will for our lives.

At the same time, we need Holy Spirit. As we grow in a depth of relationship with Holy Spirit, the Scriptures are illuminated for us, giving us deeper insight and revelation. Holy Spirit guides us and shows us how to apply the Word in a timely manner to our situations and circumstances and empowers us to do what God asks of us.

How can we know the true Spirit is speaking to us?

The first thing we need to understand is that we should not be afraid of not hearing Holy Spirit correctly. Holy Spirit always magnifies and lifts up the name and person of Jesus, Yeshua. If it glorifies Jesus, then you can believe it's from the Spirit.

After Jesus rose again, He met with the disciples in the upper room where they were hiding in great grief and fear after the death of their dear friend and teacher. In an instance, everything changed as Jesus, walking through the walls, spoke to them. Fear and trauma were replaced with the sheer joy of seeing their beloved teacher, alive and restored.

"On the evening of that day, the first day of the week, the doors being locked where the disciples were for fear of the Jews, Jesus came and stood among them and said to them, 'Peace be with you.' When he had said this, he showed them his hands and his side. Then the disciples were glad when they saw the Lord. Jesus said to them again, 'Peace be with you. As the Father has sent me, even so I am sending you.' And when he had said this, he breathed on them and said to them, 'Receive the Holy Spirit.'"[5]

But that wasn't the end of being filled with Holy Spirit. Before He ascended, on the Mount of Transfiguration, He told His disciples to go and gather in the upper room because He was going to send the Comforter, Holy Spirit, who would lead them into all truth. "And while staying with them he ordered them not to depart from Jerusalem, but to wait for the promise of the Father, which, he said, 'you heard from me; for John baptized with water, but you will be baptized with the Holy Spirit not many days from now."[6]

With baptism, the Spirit of God begins to indwell in you, regenerating and transforming you, taking your spirit from being dead to being alive in Jesus. That's the foundation for understanding the work of the Spirit. Today, many people say they are "spiritual," but biblically, being spiritual means living a life controlled by the Holy Spirit. When we're filled with the Spirit and operating in the Spirit, it largely means we're yielded to the will of God and to the Word of God. Someone who is truly spiritual will bring forth the fruit of the Spirit, which is primarily about character. Many people associate being filled with the Spirit with service to God or miraculous sign gifts, but the first evidence is character. It's reflected in how you treat people. The Spirit of God will give you the wisdom and power to overcome sin and struggles in your life, lead you into truth, and bring you into greater intimacy with the Lord. These are all aspects of what Holy Spirit does.

How do we know when it is God's voice?

Another key aspect is discerning between the Spirit of God and other voices. We have God's voice, the voice of the enemy, the voice of the world, our own inner voices, and the voices of those around us. The nature of God's voice is to build us up, not to beat us down. While there might be conviction, there will never be a sense of worthlessness or lack of value. That's the voice of the world, the flesh, or the enemy. The voice of the Lord will always guide, convict, build up, and strengthen you in your inner person. And it will always speak truth, such as in the story of the woman at the well, which I love, where Jesus says to her, "But the hour is coming, and is now here, when the true worshipers will worship the Father in spirit and truth, for the Father is seeking such people to worship him."[7]

This concept is significant because when we read, meditate, and study the Word of God, it anchors us. It tethers us to the truth. When the storms of life come, we're not swept away because we're anchored in the Word and connected to the truth. But at the same time, we need to be filled with Holy Spirit and seek Him. There must be a balance between the Word and worship. And the Word is not only the Bible, but it is the Word made flesh, which is Jesus, and knowing Him because Holy Spirit reveals Him to us. Some people are more intellectually focused, while others are more heart focused. However, there needs to be a clear connection between the head and the heart. In my journey, discovering the profound impact of seeking to be filled with the Holy Spirit helped me bridge the paths of heart and head, allowing me to truly know Jesus and stand firm on the solid ground of His truth. Let me share how this pursuit has transformed my life.

Ablaze with His Presence

As a young adult, I was swept up in a colorful era marked by the rise of trailblazers like Keith Green, Chuck Girard, and Amy Grant, who were transforming the landscape of worship music. There was a widespread move of God, and many were coming to Jesus. During this time, I had the privilege of attending a church camp meeting in Oregon, where Reinhardt Bonnke, a dynamic speaker with a mesmerizing South African accent, captivated us all.

Reinhardt spoke of the Gospel with such relevance and passion, drawing vivid pictures of Holy Spirit's power in our lives. He described the Holy Spirit not merely as a presence felt at salvation, but as a constant, overflowing source of strength—a counselor and friend who grants us wisdom. He urged us to embrace Holy Spirit fully, allowing Him to empower us daily, not just for personal salvation but as a force that enables us to live out our faith boldly and share the Gospel of Jesus with others.

His life was a testament to the power and freedom that comes from living under Holy Spirit's influence. Everywhere he went, he radiated the love of Jesus, fueled by the Spirit's healing and invigorating presence. This period was not only a time of spiritual awakening but also a season of growth, as new musicians took the stage, teaching us to worship in fresh transformative ways and to grow in our personal journeys and relationships with Jesus.

During this time, my friends had a divine encounter with Holy Spirit at the camp days earlier, and I longed for the same experience. I knew little about Holy Spirit, but I was eager to learn. My brother and I had the chance to walk up front and meet Reinhardt, but all I could think about was returning to the altar. Those were the days when going to the altar meant kneeling in reverence, acknowledging God's holiness and His welcoming love.[8]

In the back of that large building, I knelt on a thick bed of sawdust and prayed. As the room emptied around me, I stayed, determined not to leave until I was baptized in the Holy Spirit. I didn't fully understand what that meant, but seeing the passion and fire in my friends, I longed for the same. Eventually, as I persisted in prayer, a gentle sensation, like a river, bubbled up within me. Suddenly, I began speaking in another language. It was a soft and somewhat awkward experience, in the quietness of the room. In that moment, His overwhelming presence brought me to tears. That hour marked a new, deeper understanding of God for me. Time and again, I find myself marveling at the mystery of God. Those days were truly ablaze with His presence, vibrant and warm like a campfire on a summer evening.

In the midst of a generation of vibrant young believers, the experiences we shared were profoundly powerful. Whenever we prayed over people and Holy Spirit descended, I found myself enveloped in God's presence, uttering words that were not my own. This was because we were encountering Holy Spirit not just as a force, but as a person. Holy Spirit embodies presence, love, power, and the new life of God Himself, unfolding within us here and now. This transformation is not random; it happens for a reason.

Holy Spirit works within us to forge a deeper connection with God, unveiling His nature and His purposes in our lives and for those around us. God's desire is to renew us both inside and out. He guides us on a transformative journey that deepens our relationships with Him, ourselves, and others. He seeks to impart a profound understanding of His ways over our own and to refresh our spirits.

Worship and prayer help us tune in to Holy Spirit's presence, making us more aware that He is always with us. These practices don't bring Him into our presence—He's always there. Rather, they help us recognize and hear Him more clearly. Worship and prayer must come from a place of passion, love, and devotion—not just rote prayers, the singing of words, or even rote reading of the Bible. The Bible can feel like a dead book if you don't have the presence, power, and passion of Holy Spirit to bring it alive. The Word and Holy Spirit are complementary, and we need both working together in our lives—this balance of Word and worship, of study and prayer.

Remember, as Paul wrote, "If I speak in the tongues of men and of angels, but have not love, I am a noisy gong or a clanging cymbal."[9] This says that without love, our actions and gifts are meaningless.

To maintain this balance, we need to cultivate a deep, personal relationship with God through consistent spiritual disciplines. Regular time spent in prayer and worship fosters a sensitivity to Holy Spirit's guidance and prompts us to live out our faith authentically. Engaging deeply with the Bible, not just reading but meditating on its truths, allows Holy Spirit to illuminate its meaning and application in our lives.

Moreover, being a part of a community of believers can significantly enhance our spiritual journey. Fellowship with others who are also seeking to grow in their faith provides encouragement, accountability, and fresh perspectives. Together, we can experience the dynamic interaction between the Word and the Spirit in a powerful and transformative way.

In conclusion, integrating passionate worship, heartfelt prayer, diligent study of the Bible, and active participation in a faith community creates fertile ground for spiritual growth. Holy Spirit, always present, becomes more discernible and active in our daily lives. By embracing this balanced approach, we allow Holy Spirit to lead us, mold us, and empower us to live out our faith with vigor and authenticity. May we continually seek this balance and be ever receptive to the presence and prompting of Holy Spirit in all aspects of our lives.

Take some time to write in your journal.
1. *When have you felt the presence of Holy Spirit clearly in your life?*
2. *How does the Holy Spirit guide you in your daily decisions?*
3. *Reflect on a time the Holy Spirit brought healing to your heart.*

Prayer

Holy Spirit, we welcome You. We open our hearts to Your presence. We have surrendered ourselves, declaring Jesus as Lord of our lives, and now we invite You, Holy Spirit, to indwell us. Just as You dwelt in the Tabernacle in the Old Testament, we ask You to dwell within us now. May we not move until You lead us. May we remain steadfast until You direct us onward. Guide us in Your ways and help us understand the significance of our presence in the world today. Our steps, our touch, the smiles we share—let them all be impactful. If words are spoken, let them be pure and kind. Holy Spirit, fill our hearts with Your presence. We pray this in Jesus' Name. Amen.

HE WHISPERS

I listen for your whisper to lead me.

Chapter Three - He Whispers

In this chapter, we'll set out on an incredible journey up the mountain path to discover how to hear God's voice. God longs to walk with us, lighting our way along the path of life and self-discovery. As we make this spiritual climb, we'll explore the different ways God speaks to us, offering guidance, comfort, and wisdom, like a beacon on our journey. Through Scripture, personal stories, and practical exercises, you will be encouraged to open your heart to the divine whispers that can change your life. Whether just starting out or looking to deepen your connection, these lessons are crafted to help you hear God's voice more clearly and consistently, lighting your path as you move toward the summit.

From the dawn of Creation, God knew us and had a vision for our lives, recording our stories in His book. He expressed His heart for us, saying, "Let us make man in our image, after our likeness."[1] The Father envisioned us as a people who would reflect His image, His essence, His thoughts. He has always eagerly desired to communicate with us, His Creation, individually, as a community, as a nation, and as His world. Remarkably, what He sees and believes about us surpasses all our fondest imaginings. Yet, our hearts have often been inscribed with negative narratives far from His truth—those narratives we might have heard from others or have told ourselves—leading us to believe falsehoods about our identity and purpose.

We need to be reminded of His intention at the moment He breathed life into our beings within our mother's womb: "For you formed my inward parts; you knitted me together in my mother's womb. I praise you, for I am fearfully and wonderfully made. Wonderful are your works; my soul knows it very well."[2]

His profound love for us is boundless. He is eager to fill us both with the truth of our identities and His essence to empower us to achieve the heavenly objectives He has envisioned for us on this earth. The revelation of such divine love and purpose is not merely transformational but is the foundation which enables us to live in the fullness of our creation.

He Spoke from the Beginning

Imagine the beginning of time, where Father God eagerly sought to engage with us, yearning for a relationship with His Creation. Yet, when Creation recoiled in fear or dishonor, God did not retreat. Instead, He communicated through the prophets, imparting messages directly to their hearts to relay to His people.

Consider the story of Elijah, an early figure in the prophetic, who received a divine message about an impending three-year famine due to the people's disobedience.[3] God's guidance was precise: He directed Elijah to a brook for sustenance, promising that ravens would feed him daily. This narrative exemplifies God's provision for those who heed His call, illustrating His deep desire for intimate interaction with us.

As the story unfolds, the brook eventually dries up, and God instructs Elijah to go to Zarephath, where a widow is commanded to provide for him. Picture this widow, unaware of her role in God's plan, responding to a divine prompting. When Elijah encounters her at the town gate, she expresses her dire situation yet agrees to feed Elijah alongside herself and her son. Despite being a Gentile with little knowledge of Elijah's God, her willingness to give out of her great need, coupled with Elijah's obedience, results in a miraculous food supply. This fulfills God's promise that the jar of flour and jug of oil would not run dry until rain returns to the land.

Discerning His Voice

This historical account is more than a miracle; it is a testament to how God unexpectedly communicates with us. Consider those moments in your life when a job opportunity arose seemingly out of nowhere, a sermon spoke directly to your heart, or a sign appeared just when you needed direction. These "coincidences" are often divine orchestrations designed to lead us toward our destiny. God's Word, serving as a lamp to our feet and a light to our path,[4] guides us through life's journey, illuminating our path and directing us toward His purpose for our lives.

The Lord uniquely draws us into His narrative, inviting us to listen intently to His voice. Recognizing the significance of hearing from Him is crucial. God communicates in the most remarkable ways. Reflecting on my journey, there was a time during my youth when I navigated personal turmoil, seeking healing and hope. Consistent counseling and prayer ministry sessions became a lifeline, allowing me to process past wounds and connect with God on a deeper level.

During this season of restoration, I was introduced to a course titled *Communion with God*, developed by Mark and Patti Virkler.[5] The Virkler's presented a compelling approach to discerning God's voice, outlining four keys that resonated deeply within me and significantly impacted my life. Now titled *Four Keys to Hearing God's Voice*, a free, hour-long audio introduction is available online.[6]

With the addition of one, I now give you five keys to hearing God's voice—

1. Find a quiet place.

2. As you pray, fix the eyes of your heart upon Jesus. Ask God to cleanse your imagination so you can see what He wants you to see. Immanuel has always been present throughout your life, even when you were unaware.

3. Recognize that God's voice in your heart often sounds like a flow of spontaneous thoughts.

4. Engage in two-way journaling. This involves writing both your conversation with God and what you sense He is saying to you.

5. Share with a few trusted friends. This provides accountability and allows for affirmation and discernment of what you are hearing.

As we implement these steps, our spiritual ears become more attuned to His voice, leading us into deeper intimacy with Him. The foundation of this approach is to seek God with all our heart.

"You will seek me and find me when you seek me with all your heart."[7]

Being intentional and attentive in our pursuit of divine communication is paramount. When we earnestly seek to hear from God, He reveals Himself. Engaging with God in this manner is about seeking answers and fostering a deeper relationship with the Creator, who desires to speak into our brokenness and heal us. The cornerstone of my journey in hearing God's voice has always been carving out a place of stillness.

"But when you pray, go into your room, and shut the door and pray to your Father who is in secret. And your Father who sees in secret will reward you."[8]

I took this verse literally, creating prayer closets in every home I've ever lived in, transforming these spaces with elements that fostered a peaceful environment—soft lighting, worship music, perhaps a hint of essential oils, a cozy pillow, and, most importantly, my Bible and notebooks. These spaces became my refuge, especially during the demanding seasons of life as a working single mother of three.

Tucked away in these closets, a sense of quiet, simplicity, and order reigned. This ambiance minimized distractions and allowed for a focus solely on dialogue with God. I would start by calming my mind, often centering my thoughts on a single verse, dwelling on its implications, and letting its truth gently rest over me. Achieving this stillness is an active endeavor that involves consciously setting aside the whirlwind of daily tasks to tune in to God's gentle whisper.

Many times, as thoughts of pending tasks intruded upon this stillness, I'd jot them down, acknowledging their presence but postponing their urgency, so I could clear the path to engage with God without reservations. Once my mind was unburdened, I entered a place of gratitude, writing my praises in my journal.

"Enter his gates with thanksgiving, and his courts with praise! Give thanks to him; bless his name!"[9]

This approach prepared my heart for receiving and anchored me in the moment, ready to listen and perceive God's voice.

Pictures of the Mind

When Jesus walked the earth, He consistently spoke in parables, weaving spiritual truths into stories that captivated the mind and soul. This fulfilled what was spoken through the prophet:

"I will open my mouth in parables; I will utter what has been hidden since the foundation of the world."[10]

He masterfully used imagery to draw His listeners closer to the heart of God.

"With many such parables he spoke the word to them, as they were able to hear it. He did not speak to them without a parable but explained everything privately to his disciples."[11]

In my sacred times with Jesus, I emulate this concept by using my imagination, letting biblical stories and images paint vivid pictures in my mind, enriching my spiritual experience and allowing me to see beyond the words on the page to the living truth they convey.

This personal way of seeking stillness, coupled with my imagination through scriptural meditation, has deepened my connection with God. It has transformed how I perceive His voice and His presence in my life. In these moments of quiet solitude, I've experienced the most personal encounters with Him—His Word coming alive—guiding, comforting, and inspiring me. We all need this personal connection and communion with Him, both on the mountain top of our paths and the valley low.

The Shadowed Path

Imagine navigating the shadows of life's most daunting valleys, such as the loss of a child or husband, the pain of divorce, the inability to have a child, or the haunting memories of unresolved betrayals. We all face traumas that rock our world and leave us breathless. But Jesus promises that in the midst of these dark valleys, He will be there with us, providing comfort and guidance. I love the verse from Psalm 23, "Even though I walk through the valley of the shadow of death, I will fear no evil."[12] Can you remember traversing such a valley? It is then that we desperately need to hear His voice clearly—without doubt, without reservation.

The experience varies for each of us, perhaps filled with the sounds of an unknown wilderness or a forest path—a testament to the solitude of our struggles. Yet, amidst this grief and sadness, there is a comforting presence on that shadowed path. It is Immanuel, our Guide and Protector. David's poetic assurance, "Your rod and your staff, they comfort me,"[13] captures the essence of protection and guidance with profound simplicity.

David's eloquence in Psalm 23 continues to stir my heart, especially when he speaks of the Lord preparing a table before me in the presence of my enemies. Picture that table—set and waiting—a place of peace amidst conflict. At that table, in the company of Immanuel and our enemies, there exists a sacred space for forgiveness, repentance, and even the ability to forgive our adversaries. In this place, the distractions and conflicts of the world fade away, leaving only the profound truth: when we are in His presence, we find our truest selves, embraced, and understood, with His whispering voice filling us.

This journey of faith, marked by moments of fearlessness in the face of adversity and profound peace amidst turmoil, is not just about enduring trials but about the transformation occurring within us as we walk through it, hand in hand with Immanuel, learning to tune to His voice. Our imaginations play a crucial role in this spiritual journey, allowing us to see beyond the immediate to the eternal, to envision not just the challenges before us but the steadfast presence of Jesus guiding us through with His quiet whisper. Immanuel, God with us. David's psalm reminds us that our faith is not just a series of beliefs but a vivid, deeply personal narrative we live out daily.

By My Side

In my daily walk, I've made it a practice to look to Him, quieting my soul: "Lord, I'm just focusing on You ..." and drawing on the unshakeable promise, knowing He's always right here covers us with a sense of security:

"I will never leave you nor forsake you."[14]

My experiences of His presence are tangible and deeply personal. Sometimes, as I drive, I imagine Jesus sitting in the passenger seat, journeying alongside me. In those moments, a simple "Thank You for being here" profoundly acknowledges His reality in my life. Similarly, my visits to Cannon Beach, Oregon—a place that holds a special place in my heart—have been highlights of these personal encounters. As I cross the bridge leading to the sand, I feel a deep sense of peace descending upon me. Once, I found myself dozing off under the warmth of the sun, the sand beneath acting as a cradle of rest. In my heart, I knew Jesus was there with me, as real as the sun and the sand.

In that moment, I found myself pouring out my heart to Him, sharing all my worries about my children, grandchildren, and husband. I needed His wisdom to know which burdens to carry and which to lay at His feet. The beauty of these moments is how His guidance comes—spontaneous thoughts that seem to speak directly into my circumstances, offering clarity and direction.

As I sat there, talking to Him about my concerns, I could feel His voice responding with such love and compassion. When I looked up, I felt as if I could see His face, gently caring for my worries and my heart. He reassured me that He would lead me and guide me through this season. He promised to constantly teach me, give me wisdom and light my path. I'm so grateful to feel His presence, always there, letting me know I'm never alone.

The culmination of these divine encounters is found in writing them down. Whether they're visions or simply the stirrings of my imagination where I see myself meeting with God, each word penned is a testament to His presence and voice in my life. This practice isn't just about record-keeping; it's a way to cherish and revisit the moments God speaks:

"Write the vision; make it plain on tablets, so he may run who reads it."[15]

Through these narratives, my journey with Jesus becomes a story rich with His Presence, a testament to how He reveals Himself and guides me. It's a path marked by heartfelt dialogues, serene encounters on sandy beaches, and the quiet assurance that God is with us in every moment, weaving our stories into His grand tapestry of love and purpose.

Dreams

As He did in the Old Testament, giving warnings and direction, God still communicates with us through dreams. I'm particularly drawn to this method because it's beyond my control. While asleep, in a state of vulnerability, dreams come, encased in various forms. In some, I'm merely an observer, and in others, I'm an active participant. These dreams might be personal or intended for someone else, showcasing God's diverse speaking methods.

I have a fondness for simply watching the dreams unfold. For those curious to explore the meanings behind their dreams, I've found great insight in resources such as those by John Paul Jackson[16] and Streams Ministry[17] on dream interpretation, Mark Virkler's teachings on Hearing God through your Dreams[18] and Barbie Breathitt's extensive dream encyclopedia.[19] These authors offer tools for deciphering the divine messages woven into our nighttime visions, enriching our spiritual journey. Such tools offer interpretations and invite us closer to God, revealing His whispers at night.

As I prepare for sleep, my prayer is a simple invitation: "Lord Jesus, I welcome Your presence." Although it's not a nightly ritual, I intend always to remain open to the Holy Spirit's guidance. With gratitude, I lay down to rest, entrusting my spirit to God's peace, regardless of the world's turmoil. "Come close, Holy Spirit," I pray, yearning for divine revelations through dreams and visions, seeking clarity and remembrance to pen down these night whispers.

There are nights when awakenings bring revelations, moments I hastily capture through voice recordings, honoring the sacredness of God's communication. This practice is about retaining messages and showing reverence for His approach to speaking into my life. Ignoring these divine moments risks silencing His voice, or even worse, muting my ability to hear—a risk I'm unwilling to take.

He guides us on paths of righteousness, a journey illuminated by His presence and voice, even in the stillness of night.

"He restores my soul. He leads me in paths of righteousness for his name's sake."[20]

In embracing this, my sleep becomes more than rest; it transforms into a sacred space for divine encounter and guidance. It is God speaking to me. And I am learning to hear His voice.[21]

He wants to guide us through so much of our lives. And right now, in the generation we're living in, we will see some of the most spectacular, incredible things. The blind will see, the deaf will hear, the lame will walk; and the dead will rise again. As Jesus had said to His disciples,

"Truly, truly, I say to you, whoever believes in me will also do the works that I do; and greater works than these will he do, because I am going to the Father."[22]

I am longing for the greater—and for everything we were meant to be as we trust in the guiding light of God's Word, echoed from long ago through the voice of the psalmist:

"Your word is a lamp to my feet and a light to my path...."[23]

Encouraging Words

Embracing the gift of prophecy is another one of the profound ways we connect with God's voice. This echoes the sentiment of Paul, who expressed, "I wish that you all may prophesy,"[24] drawing attention to the importance of uplifting and calling forth the potential in others and confirming it in their own hearts.

My journey to understanding this came during a pivotal moment around my 40th birthday—a time marked by a desperate quest for freedom from nightmares and fears that had plagued me for decades. Like David pouring out his heart in the Psalms, I learned to take time to write down my requests to God. In the dawn of the year 2001, I found myself seated, journal in hand, pouring my heart out. With a fervent plea, I sought freedom, expressing my exhaustion over the fear that had held me captive—fear birthed from haunting childhood memories and an unease that lurked in the shadows. Night after night, I would recheck my doors, ensuring they were locked, never once sleeping without the comforting glow of a bedside light. My soul was plagued by fears and anxieties.

It was during these moments of vulnerability that the Lord infused a spontaneous thought that spoke a prophetic word within me—a gentle but profound revelation. I wrote in the journal, "Rochelle, you do not grasp the extent of your chains, but soon, after you are free, you will realize the depth of your captivity and you will know that I brought you freedom." When the Lord speaks of 'soon,' it can still signify a lengthy wait. However, in my journey, His promise materialized swiftly. Within a few months, I found myself in the company of my prayer ministers—and God profoundly encountered us. He liberated me with astonishing swiftness, shattering the chains that had me bound. As I opened my eyes, an overwhelming sense of freedom washed over me; I knew without a doubt that the freedom He had promised was now my reality. In the chapters to come, I look forward to sharing that transformative story with you.

Following that liberating experience, the Lord guided me toward nurturing the prophetic gift within me. He encouraged me to share uplifting and encouraging words with others, teaching me the importance of this practice in my spiritual journey.

Paul's encouragement for all to prophesy is a reminder of the power of speaking life into others' journeys.[25] It's about more than just hearing God for ourselves; it's about being conduits of encouragement, hope, and affirmation as we hear God for one another. As we meet, whether in gatherings or daily interactions, we're invited to practice this gift, to speak over each other's lives, fostering an environment where the prophetic can flourish, not for our glory but for God's glory and the encouragement of His people.

The Scripture reminds us not to neglect this gathering together, for in such assemblies, we are called to teach and encourage one another,[26] singing songs of faith and sharing God's Word. Within these gatherings, we can hear God's voice more clearly and support each other's spiritual journey. These community experiences are vital in deepening our understanding of God's will and reinforcing our faith.

Taking time to nurture your gifting is vital. I often say, "When I look at you, this is what I see," to highlight the unseen virtues and gifts in others. This practice is about observing and recognizing people's positive impact, much like capturing their essence through a video camera of which they are unaware. It's about affirming the sacred light they bring into a room or the love they shower on others. For instance, I recently shared with someone how their kindness and compassionate heart toward others was so lovely, emphasizing the superhero anointing gift they possess. Encouraging each other builds up all of us. (And it is so fun!)

Divine Encounters and Miraculous Intervention

As we learn to hear God's voice and walk with Him, encountering Him deeper and deeper, it will be challenging. We often receive miracles when our circumstances dictate that we need one! But through these trials, we will hear His voice in the miracles and surprises He opens up before us. We may believe to some extent, but our faith and belief heighten—thus the tuning of our ear to His voice improves—as we experience the depths of God's love found in the divine encounters and the miracles He provides.

Through our difficulties, God assures us of His presence in tangible manners, often through meeting our physical and emotional needs. We see this unfold in Scripture, for both Elijah and the widow of Zarephath. In 1 Kings 17:4-6, God commanded the ravens to feed Elijah. Similarly, in 1 Kings 17:9, He guided the widow, unaware of His divine intervention, to supply sustenance for Elijah.

This supernatural guidance becomes evident as the widow interacts with Elijah, a man of faith. However, tragedy strikes when her son falls ill, deteriorates, and eventually stops breathing. Distraught, she confronts Elijah, asking, "What do you have against me, man of God? Did you come to remind me of my sin and kill my son?"[27]

Such moments of adversity reveal our deepest beliefs and fears. In her despair, she questioned if God was punishing her, revealing a struggle to reconcile her understanding of God's nature with her circumstances. Yet, the narrative highlights God's patience and kindness. God had orchestrated a profound encounter for her amidst a tragic moment that would transform her belief system. Elijah, acting as God's emissary, said, "Give me your son." He then took the boy from her arms, brought him to the upper room where he was staying, and laid him on his bed. In desperation, Elijah cried out to the Lord, "O Lord my God, have you brought calamity even upon the widow with whom I sojourn by killing her son?"[28] The woman, a Gentile unfamiliar with the ways of God, was about to witness the power of the God of Israel. Elijah stretched out over the boy three times, fervently praying, "O Lord my God, let this child's life come into him again."[29] God heard Elijah's cry, and the boy's life was restored.

Elijah then brought the boy down to his mother and declared, "See, your son lives."[30] This miraculous event led the woman to proclaim, "Now I know that you are a man of God and that the word of the Lord in your mouth is truth."[31] This divine intervention demonstrates God's power and loving-kindness, challenging and transforming her misconceptions and teaching a lesson of faith and grace that will leave an indelible mark on her heart. She now believes, without doubt, that she can trust the voice of the Lord.

Just as the widow's experience transformed her understanding of God's character, so too can our encounters with Him rekindle hope and renew our spirit. God's intervention breathes life into our circumstances, affirming that He is indeed "Immanuel," God with us—whispering right into our hearts—and sovereign over all.

In my role on the altar team at my church, praying for people is a privilege. When they seek prayer, I sometimes shift toward inviting Jesus into our midst, asking, "Can we invite Jesus to reveal what He wants to say to you?" This opens a space for these divine encounters, allowing individuals to hear directly from Jesus about their concerns, whether it concerns family, job struggles, personal loss, or other deep matters of the heart.

Encouraging people to perceive Jesus' presence and message often reveals His amazing love and intention to assist them, differing significantly from any negative portrayal. Such experiences can sincerely affirm and heal in ways beyond what our words alone can achieve.

As you continue on this path, remember to document your journaling of hearing God's voice. This practice serves as a conduit for growth and encouragement in your spiritual journey. Validating each other's spiritual insights, aligning them with Scripture, and fortifying our understanding of God's intentions is a profound privilege. It is wise to find at least three trusted friends with whom you can share your journaling. Ask them if they sense what you are hearing is from God as you increase your discernment in hearing His voice. Remember, there is wisdom in a multitude of counselors.

As we conclude this chapter, let us embrace the journey of seeking God's whispers in our lives. Through personal reflection, small gatherings, and the shared wisdom of trusted friends, we can cultivate a deeper connection with God. May we continue to open our hearts to His presence, allowing His voice to guide us through life's valleys and peaks. In this journey we find strength, comfort, and assurance that God is always with us, lighting our path and leading us toward His divine purpose.

Let us quiet ourselves, listen to our hearts and imagination, and tune in to the flow of His thoughts. As we do so, may we write down what we hear, fostering a deeper awareness of His presence in our lives.
Take some time to write in your journal.
1. *Reflect on a time you felt your purpose was clear. How di that align with God's plan for you?*
2. *What pain or betrayal do you need to surrender to Jesus for healing?*
3. *How can you use your past experiences to help guide others?*

Prayer to Cleanse Our Imagination

Lord, we pray for a heightened awareness of Your workings around us, ears attuned to Your voice in all its subtleties, and hearts sensitive to the needs of others. May we be instruments of encouragement and bearers of Your light, reflecting Your love in every aspect of our lives.

Lord, cleanse our eyes, ears, mouth, and heart. Guide our gaze toward You, Jesus. We are thankful to the Holy Spirit for leading us to discover Jesus and understand the Father more deeply. We offer our hearts and lives to You, asking for Your guidance and the ability to hear Your voice clearly. Help us to hear only You, and confirm Your voice through Scripture, random situations, and even through others, so we may understand what You are saying. Teach us to trust in the counsel You provide so we may grasp the full picture of Your calling and destiny for our lives.

In Jesus' name, Amen.

TELL HER STORY

Where there is **imperfection**
There Is an abundance of **beauty.**

Chapter Four - Tell Her Story

We overcome by the power of His blood and the word of our testimony. Throughout my journey of faith in Jesus, I've felt a deep connection with many women in the Bible, like Esther, Deborah, and Lydia. However, I noticed that in my deepest pain and sorrow, I found my heart aligning more with those who had battled the same fears and wounds that I did, such as the woman at the well or the one breaking the alabaster jar. These women were not perfect, yet Jesus met each of them with a love that freed them from their sins and restored them to life. Their stories inspired me to keep going.

As we share pieces of our stories, we embrace the message that the Lord is unlocking our voices and giving us back our songs. Sharing our stories can be intimidating; many of us have practiced hiding our true selves, presenting only the parts we deem "acceptable." Deep down, fear whispers, "If you really know me, you won't love me," or "I'm too much, and if I share too much, you'll leave."

These are the very areas in which Jesus works to bring breakthrough, turning our mourning into dancing and our silence into singing:

"The Lord your God is in your midst, a mighty one who will save; he will rejoice over you with gladness; he will quiet you by his love; he will exult over you with loud singing."[1]

It is a privilege to explore our sacred stories together, discovering how, when Jesus encounters us, He not only changes our narrative but empowers us to reclaim our voice and sing our redeemed song. This is the encouragement and life-changing power of meeting the King of Kings, His son Yeshua, and the Holy Spirit. We need to be reminded, and others need to know that He is our Deliverer, our Healer. He sees us and knows us; He lifts the shame off us and makes space for us to believe in His hope. "For with God nothing will be impossible."[2]

With Jesus, we can move every impossible thing out of our way. Much like moving mountains, He takes the impossible and makes it possible. He takes the broken, insignificant, and unwanted and transforms their lives into the most beautiful story.

We believe that your story could be just what others need to hear to strengthen their faith and continue their spiritual journey. Let's explore a few stories from the Bible and how they relate to Jesus' teachings.

Mary Magdalene

I am Mary Magdalene, and through my eyes, I have witnessed marvels that words can barely convey. My story begins not with who I was but with the profound encounter I had with Yeshua. In my darkest moments, when fear and depression gripped me tightly, He came to where I was in the darkest place and, without hesitation, demanded my demons leave. He was relentless in His desire to see me free. His touch did more than heal; it filled me with a deep love and gratitude for what I could never have done for myself. He chose to love me and free me before I could ever give Him anything in return.

I emerged from the cage of my addictions, generational iniquities, and the spirit of death, completely changed by His light and love. I had no strength to seek Him, yet He sought me out and freed me with a love that changed everything.

As the days passed, I saw Him free so many others. His words, "I came to seek and save the lost," profoundly inspired me. His actions taught me to love in a deep and meaningful way. As He said, those who are forgiven much, love much. This truth reshaped my heart, helping me to embrace a life filled with purpose and hope.

I was not merely an onlooker in His journey; I actively participated, supporting His ministry alongside other devoted men and women. Together, we were integral to a movement that healed the blind, enabled the deaf to hear, and helped the lame to walk. We fed the hungry and broke the chains of tyranny, all through His powerful name.

When I was at the tomb, I was filled with grief as I found it empty. I was startled out of my thoughts by the sound of a man asking who I was looking for. I had no idea who He was until He spoke my name—Mary. I responded, it was my risen Savior. My heart was ecstatic with joy, but He told me, "Go tell the rest I have risen. I am alive."

This hope ignited within me a burning zeal that endures to this day. Amidst the solitude and trauma of witnessing His agony, He appeared to me, entrusting me with the crucial task of proclaiming His resurrection and the lasting hope that our journey continues. His request was not only a recognition of my faith but also an empowerment for all who would come to believe through my words. My story is a testament to His grace. He brings freedom, fills our lives with purpose, and triumphs over darkness.

My story is meant to touch hearts, spark hope, and light the way for others so they too, may find and believe in Him. He enters our darkness to rescue us. He brings light and tears down the walls built around our hearts by lies we once believed, transforming our lives from lost to overflowing with abundance. Jesus frees us and fills our lives with profound purpose. He breaks the curse of darkness and the generational reaping of sins passed down. Life is restored to our original design. The enemy does not hold ultimate control; God's power triumphs, freeing us from darkness and transforming our stories into beacons of hope and support for others.

Two Daughters (Mark 5:25-29)

A Morning of Miracles

The hushed dawn of a day destined to be remembered was laden with the sweet scent of hope, despite the undercurrent of my own silent suffering. My life, until then, had been a relentless battle against an ailment that left me financially ruined and socially isolated, marked as 'unclean' and untouchable.

But that morning, whispers of a healer whose very name made the dark shadows tremble ignited a fragile spark of hope within me. Despite the cultural norms that shunned my presence, the chance to merely be near Him compelled me forward. With a heart pounding with both fear and anticipation, I set out with a simple plan: to discreetly touch the hem of His garment as He passed by, hoping to remain unseen.

This touch, so light yet so charged, was to be my final chance after years of fruitless treatments. My condition not only inflicted physical pain but also estranged me from my family—no shared meals, no warm embraces, not even the casual brush of hands. My very presence was a burden of impurity to them. I was lonely and felt lost without purpose. Little did I know that all of this was about to change.

As I weaved through the crowd that fateful morning, low to the ground, my fingers barely caught the hem of His garment. In that instant, a surge of healing power flowed through me, as real and as startling as a burst of sunlight through dark clouds. He stopped. "Who touched Me?" His voice echoed through the crowd. Panic and relief flooded me in equal measure as I realized I could no longer hide.

When His eyes met mine, I felt a warmth of love and a smile of acceptance so real that my trembling ceased. I fell to His feet, and He touched me. He spoke gently, "Daughter, be of good comfort: your faith has made you whole." Those words not only restored my body but all of my humanity—body, soul, and spirit.

Just then, a desperate father, Jairus, approached, openly begging for his daughter's life—a stark contrast to my hidden approach. As Jesus moved to help him, I witnessed the depth of Jesus' compassion unfold. Yet, our renewed hope was briefly overshadowed by the devastating news of the young girl's passing. Amidst the grief, Jesus' unwavering words to Jairus, "Do not fear—just keep trusting, and she will be restored," brought comfort and strength.

At Jairus' home, surrounded by mourners, Jesus commanded the young girl to rise, boldly defying the power of death. The room, filled with despair moments before, bloomed into an arena of joy as life was restored to the young child.

Our intertwined stories of miraculous healing and resurrection have forever changed my life, and that of many others. They serve as a powerful testament to the transformative strength of faith in Jesus. He reaches into our deepest despair to offer not only healing but a profound peace and freedom that surpasses all understanding.

When we reach out to Jesus in our pain and brokenness, He faithfully meets us with healing and addresses our deepest needs, speaking peace and freedom into our lives.

Samaritan Woman (John 4:5-30)

I am the woman of Samaria, who encountered Jesus by the well during the fiercest heat of the day. Historically, this well had witnessed declarations from three or four kings; they had proclaimed that God would be honored, yet one notably chose to disobey God at this same well. Jesus' presence at this well was not only about a personal restoration but was symbolic of renewing the land itself and to declare He was the Messiah.

He asked me for a drink, initiating a conversation that unveiled the interesting concept of Living Water—a gift so transformative that it promised to quench not only physical thirst but also the deeper, spiritual thirsts. It was a conversation that opened my eyes to my own spiritual needs.

As we spoke, it became evident that He knew everything about my life, yet His depth of knowledge came without any hint of judgment. Instead, He extended an invitation to embrace a new beginning. This encounter didn't just transform my own life; it propelled me to share the news with my entire community, leading many to believe in Him as well.

The truth I learned that day, which still resonates deeply within me, is that God knows us completely—our past, our present, and our future—and still He offers us hope, forgiveness, and a new beginning. His knowledge is not for condemnation but for redemption. The change He ignited in my heart has the power to draw whole communities to His grace and truth.

God is all-knowing and all-forgiving. He restores and redeems us and heals us spiritually. The transformation He sparks within us can inspire and draw an entire community closer to Him.

Peter's Mother-in-Law (Matt 8:14-15)

I am Peter's mother-in-law, and my story is a simple one of miraculous healing and love. On a day when fever gripped me tightly, burning me from the inside, I lay weak and weary in my home. While others might have kept their distance, fearing the sickness, Jesus walked in with a calm and caring presence.

He came straight to my side and with a gentle touch, as soothing as a cool wind on a hot day, He lifted me up. The fever that had overwhelmed me melted away instantly. In that moment, not only was my body healed, but my spirit was filled with a new energy and light.

Feeling strong and grateful, I arose from my bed. There was no obligation, only a deep desire to serve Him who had healed me so completely. It wasn't just my health that He restored; He also refreshed my heart and soul. His kindness and the peace He brought were unlike anything I had ever felt.

This experience showed me who Jesus really is. He knows our struggles and steps right into our lives with healing and hope. His touch that day wasn't just about getting better; it was an invitation for a fresh start. The healing I received inspired me to share His kindness and strength with others.

This simple truth stays with me always: God's love is personal and life changing. Through His actions, we see that He cares deeply, not just for us, but for our families and all those around us. Jesus showed me that day that in His eyes, no one is ever forgotten or beyond hope.

Jesus is a restorer of strength and holds all power. He heals us and calls us to "get up" and move forward. He places us where we can use our gifts to bless and assist others, engaging us in the ministries He has prepared for us.

Daughter of Abraham (Luke 12:10-17)

For eighteen years, I carried the weight of a burden that bent my body and tried my spirit. Every day, my stooped figure was a visible mark of my struggles, a symbol of endurance in the face of relentless physical pain and affliction. Yet, despite my constraints, my heart remained devoted, and I continued to worship. On one beautiful Sabbath, within the sacred walls of the synagogue, my life took a miraculous turn.

As I stood there, crooked, and weary, Jesus, the compassionate teacher, saw me—not as a broken thing needing pity, but as a daughter of Abraham deserving freedom. He called me to come forward, and with a voice that wrapped around my pain like a warm embrace, He declared, "Woman, you are set free." As He laid His hands on me, a strength I hadn't felt in nearly two decades surged through my veins. I straightened up, my spine realigning with a swift, graceful motion as if it had never known deformity. Overwhelmed with joy, my voice rose in praise, echoing off the synagogue walls, a spontaneous outburst of gratitude to God.

Yet not everyone shared in this joy. The leader of the synagogue, bound by tradition and rule, condemned the healing simply because it had occurred on the Sabbath. But Jesus, with calm authority, challenged this narrow view, questioning why I, a daughter of Abraham, should not be freed from bondage on a day meant for holiness and rest. His wise words quelled the critics and stirred awe among the onlookers.

This profound encounter taught me that God's timing is impeccable, His ways inscrutable. He sees our suffering, understands our needs, and chooses the perfect moment for our deliverance. This story, my story, serves as a testament to God's boundless grace. It reminds us that where there is oppression, God brings freedom; where there is brokenness, He offers healing. You too, must continue to trust in God's power to straighten what is bent and to reveal His glory through your restoration season.

God's timing might not always align with our expectations—sometimes, it may even seem slow. But God is intimately aware of our struggles and intricately involved in our stories. Let Him transform your trials into triumphs and your pain into praise. What may appear as malevolent intent from others, God can repurpose for good. Continue to trust in His unfailing ability to uplift you. He will straighten what's been bent and glorify Himself through your restoration.

Woman Caught in Adultery (John 8:1-11)

 In the dusty streets of Jerusalem, I found myself ensnared not only by my own actions but by those eager to use me as a pawn in a larger scheme to challenge Jesus. They dragged me before Him and the crowd, my heart pounding outside my chest, my shame exposed for all to see. As stones clenched in judgmental hands awaited His command, the air was thick with my fear and their anticipation.

Then, He knelt and wrote silently in the sand—a quiet movement against the clamor of condemnation. His response, gentle yet profound, echoed: "Let he who is without sin cast the first stone." One by one, the stones dropped, thudding softly against the earth, the crowd dissipating as each person was confronted with their own imperfection.

When we were alone, His eyes met mine, "Where are your accusers?" My eyes looked away but gently His gaze pulled me back as I saw in them not disdain but infinite compassion. He spoke, "Neither do I condemn you; go and leave your life of sin," His words were a soothing balm, healing the wounds of condemnation and rejection. He offered me not just forgiveness, but a new path steeped in hope and renewal.

As I walked away, His admonition birthed a hope within me. The possibility of a life reimagined, where I was no longer defined by my worst moments, seemed tangible. In following His path, I found a refuge from disgrace, a peaceful sanctuary in the strength of His forgiveness. This encounter, where incredible mercy met a broken spirit, transformed me—my testimony to the transformative power of grace that I carry in my heart forever.

Jesus comes to mend our spiritual wounds and liberate us from our sins. He is our pathway through the impossible. He is our Rescuer and our Protector. If today finds you weighed down by anxiety, sin, or turmoil, lift your eyes to Jesus. He is ready to forgive and offer grace, encouraging you to rise, move forward, and find strength in His presence.

The Alabaster Jar (Luke 7:37-38)

One of my favorite female characters in the Bible is a woman who remains unnamed. Her story unfolds when Jesus visits Simon the Leper. She enters and breaks open a flask of costly and exquisite perfume, anointing Jesus' feet.

In the quiet town of Bethany, I held my most precious possession—an alabaster jar filled with expensive oil of pure nard. With a heart heavy yet resolute, I approached the house of Simon the leper, where Yeshua was dining. Despite my checkered past, no one could have foreseen my bold entry into that gathering of men.

As I knelt beside Yeshua, the weight of my past sins and the scorn of my community bore down on me, yet my focus remained clear. With tears streaming down my face, I broke the seal of the alabaster jar and poured the fragrant oil upon His feet, an act of deep love, gratitude, and devotion as I gave my most valued possession to Him. The room filled with the scent of the oil, a fragrance I will never forget, as it spoke of honor and impending sorrow.

The reaction was swift and harsh. Disciples and guests alike were indignant, their words sharp: "Why this waste? This could have been sold and the money given to the poor!" Their voices rose in a chorus of disapproval, their rebuke stinging like the chill of winter.

But Yeshua, with a calm that silenced the room, defended me. "Why do you trouble this woman? She has done a beautiful thing to Me. For you always have the poor with you, but you will not always have Me. In pouring this ointment on My body, she has done it to prepare Me for burial." His words were an ointment, turning scorn into sacred silence. He then proclaimed, "Truly, I say to you, wherever this Gospel is proclaimed in the whole world, what she has done will also be told in memory of her."

And so, my simple, heartfelt act was woven into the eternal tapestry of His story. Each drop of oil was a testament to my repentance, my respect, and my profound belief in Him as my Savior. In that moment, Yeshua lifted me from the shadow of my past, honoring my actions as part of a greater plan. My offering, meant for Him, became a symbol of unmeasured forgiveness and grace, a reminder that in Yeshua, there is boundless love and redemption for all, even for one like me, who was once lost but now found.

There is boundless love and redemption available through Him, and genuine repentance opens the door to divine forgiveness and renewal.

Rochelle's Story: The Silent Battle

My childhood was a paradox. Every Sunday, my family sat in the front pews of our church, dressed impeccably and smiling brightly at fellow parishioners. Yet, behind the closed doors of our home, an entirely different narrative unfolded. It was a world of chaos and unpredictability, woven together by the unresolved traumas of my parents' pasts.

By the time my mother was twenty-four, she had given birth to five children, with ages spanning ten years from oldest to youngest. She was a woman of contradictions, capable of motherly love and warmth, yet often disappearing into a maze of her own mind. Diagnosed much later in life with schizophrenia, my mother battled a myriad of inner demons born from her history of abuse and trauma. This tumult manifested in episodes where she vanished for days in a sickbed or literally left the home, leaving my brothers and me to fend for ourselves. When she reappeared, she was sometimes disheveled and distant, other times the nurturing mother we all desperately needed. Life with her was a relentless roller coaster, each day unpredictable and fraught with danger.

My father was a man of passive devotion. He adored my mother, entranced by her beauty and charisma, yet equally entrapped by her darker, oppressive sides. His compliance, even when it led to harm for my brothers and me, added to my confusion and fear. This duality in my parents set the stage for a childhood shadowed by uncertainty and tension, my nights haunted by fear and anxiety.

Amidst the turmoil, my mother would occasionally sit by our beds and read stories of great missionaries like Corrie Ten Boom, Father Andrew, and Nicky Cruz. These stories offered a glimpse of hope and faith, but the stark contrast between the tales of heroism and the chaos of our home life deepened my internal struggle. My spiritual journey became a battlefield, as unpredictable and complex as my mother's shifting moods.

I sought solace in my walk-in closet, my sanctuary amidst the chaos. I would hide there in the dark, hoping to be invisible while the household erupted in screams and upheaval. It was a fragile refuge where I could momentarily escape the storm brewing outside.

Whenever things spiraled out of control, I would be angry at God, questioning the divine fairness of my circumstances. "Don't you see me and how hard I'm working to try to be good?" I would plead. "Can't you see that I'm trying to obey everything You say so that You will bring blessings and positive things into my life?" When I couldn't blame God, I would quickly turn my anger inward, directing it at myself when I could no longer bear it. I judged myself harshly, convinced there was something fundamentally wrong with me, something I could never fix. What I yearned for most was to be seen and understood, to be loved for who I truly was, beyond the tumult that defined my existence. I longed for a family that embodied the stability and love I had never known.

But once the anger subsided, I would fall back into the familiar pattern of striving for goodness, a cycle that entrapped me in its demands. My unyielding quest for perfection became its own form of captivity. I rarely rocked the boat, trying to make life easier for my parents and shield my family from external judgment. I focused on getting good grades, graduating early, and obeying my parents. The unspoken rule was simple: don't tell. Nobody outside our home knew the depth of the chaos within.

In my heart, I nurtured the hope of finding peace in the middle of the storm, of breaking free from the chains of my life and discovering a place where I could be truly myself, seen, known, and loved. My journey was a quiet resilience, a silent battle fought in the shadows, striving for light and healing in a world that often seemed to conspire against me.

Then, at age fourteen, my prayers were answered. A loving pastor's wife noticed me in a new church community we visited, hugged me for the first time, and let me know she was so glad that I was there. Her hug and kiss on my cheek changed my heart forever. Jesus used her to love me and to open a space in my heart to believe there was something redeeming about who I was. I remember saying to myself, "If this is what love looks like, I am staying here forever."

In the same church community, I was blessed with the most wonderful youth pastors who genuinely cared for me. They invited me into their family, offering me a glimpse of a life unmarked by dysfunction. Although they never directly addressed the issues in my home, I later realized they must have recognized the signs. In their gentle and caring way, they truly saved my life by inviting me into their family and calling me their daughter. They included me in family trips and met my needs by surrounding me with love and care. They also provided me with a safe space where I could talk to someone and feel truly loved. This nurturing environment helped me heal and kept me in my journey of faith, allowing Jesus to rescue me.

Through this experience, I learned that no matter how far we've strayed or how broken our circumstances may be, God wants to heal us. He often uses those who have already been healed to aid in our healing, and this transformation occurs within a supportive community. I believe this is why I am so passionate about helping others find freedom. Jesus found and rescued me when I was lost, and I am committed to sharing that same hope with others.

As I navigated the complexities of my upbringing, I discovered that true freedom lay not in being perfect but in embracing my own story, flawed and beautiful, and finding the courage to be myself amidst it all.

Reflecting on the journey from those shadowed beginnings to the liberating expanses of faith, I recognize the hand of the Savior guiding me through every trial and triumph. The voices of doubt and fear have been replaced by the affirming voice of Jesus, consistently whispering truths of love and freedom into my heart. With each step forward, the chains of my past lose their grip, allowing me to walk in the fullness of who I was created to be. This story of transformation is not just mine to tell but a testimony to the power of the unwavering faith and the relentless pursuit of the One who promises true liberty. My heart overflows with gratitude for every moment of divine intervention, knowing that in the embrace of my Heavenly Father, I am forever safe, loved, and free. Each chapter of this journey, vividly etched in the corridors of my memory, stands as a light of hope and a declaration that indeed, where the Spirit of the Lord is, there is freedom.

Hearing the stories of women who encountered Jesus—how His love and favor transformed their lives—might inspire you to share your own journey. Do you see how your story could impact another, helping them believe that God cares for even the smallest details? Every piece of your story helps unravel the mystery of how your life influences others, be it your family, your partner, your community, or even your nation.

First, though, it's crucial to reflect on your own narrative. Wrestle with it. Ask the right questions: What beliefs did my heart hold in those moments? Am I living in alignment with what Jesus says about who I am, or have I let circumstances define me? Jesus is adept at untangling pain, trauma, and shame, carrying our fears, anxieties, and burdens to the cross. In exchange, He offers us a new robe of righteousness. This transformation not only helps us rediscover the original song within us—the melody that was ours before the world's noise and harsh words dimmed its tune—but it also restores a song of hope, a vibrant chorus that resounds with the promise of renewal and redemption.

Just like the women we've discussed, whose stories evolved from invisibility and brokenness to recognition and understanding, you too have a powerful tale to tell. He saw them, knew them, and understood them— and they were just right for Him, perfectly placed within His narrative of love. Their journeys of newfound faith and hope weave a path for others to follow, encouraging them to uncover their own destinies through the power of shared experiences, and to sing the song that has been in their hearts since the beginning of time. And now, through His love, the song will return ... vibrant and filled with hope.

Take some time to write in your journal.
   1. *What is a significant part of your story that you feel called to share?*

HEART OF THE
ARCHER

Trust in the Lord completely, and do not rely on your own opinions. With all your heart rely on him to guide you, and he will lead you in every decision you make. Become intimate with him in whatever you do, and he will lead you wherever you go.

Proverbs 3:5-6 (TPT)

Chapter Five: Heart of the Archer

Those moments when a word strikes your heart to its depth—those are "arrows." In Psalms 18:14, David celebrates the God of our salvation and introduces this concept with his words, "He sent out His arrows and scattered the enemy." This powerful imagery displays how our lives are influenced by these arrows—both our own intentions and the actions and influences of others.

In this chapter, we explore the concept of "arrows" in our lives, symbolizing the direction we choose and the forces that impact us. These arrows represent the target of our energy and intentions, as well as the influences and challenges we face from others. We'll delve into the importance of aligning our beliefs with God's truth, confronting and healing from past traumas, and embracing our true identity in Christ. Through personal stories and biblical insights, we'll see how God transforms our pain into purpose, enabling us to become beacons of light in the world, starting with ourselves.

Just as a warrior carefully aims and releases each arrow, we must be intentional about where we aim our focus and how we respond to the arrows aimed at us. Our choices and reactions have their own paths and purposes, and if approached with prayer and intention, they can achieve remarkable things.

As we consider the role of prayer, it becomes clear that praying about everything is crucial. By allowing Holy Spirit to be the leader in our lives, we can seek divine guidance to better discern the paths we should take and the ways we can positively influence the world around us. With prayer, we can ensure that our arrows hit the mark, fulfilling their intended purpose in God's plan.

If you haven't yet embraced Jesus or invited Him to be the Lord of your life, I really encourage you to do so. It's crucial for this journey. You can't fully become who you're meant to be without the Creator being Lord of your life, and there's no other way to truly heal. There are no shortcuts or alternative routes. Around the world, people are seeking all sorts of ways to mend their hearts and fulfill their purpose. We were created in His image with a deep desire to be purposeful and to accomplish amazing things. We hunger for our true design to emerge. Yet, without the Creator being at the center, it falls short. I long to see you rise into all that you're meant to be.

As I reflect on my own journey, I realize how vital this truth has been in my life. The last few years have been incredibly tough for me. I thought I was on the right path, that my arrow was hitting the mark, aimed right at the target. It felt like I had a bullseye on the target of my purpose, that I was finally on my way to fulfilling exactly what I've been created for. Since those young years, I felt destined for something that would help set the captives free. One of my favorite chapters in the Bible is Isaiah 61, which beautifully speaks about this: "The Spirit of the Lord God is upon me, because the Lord has anointed me to bring good news to the poor; he has sent me to bind up the brokenhearted, to proclaim liberty to the captives, and the opening of the prison to those who are bound"[1]

I felt like I was made for a purpose, right in the center of something meaningful. But then everything went haywire. Betrayals, challenges with my shortcomings—all of it played a part. I ended up feeling lost and deeply hurt. I didn't want to leave my house; I remember nights spent in tears. There were other experiences of betrayal, like friendships that ended abruptly without explanation, and accusations and misunderstandings that circulated but never gave me the opportunity to speak my truth.

Added to the unraveling, my husband became seriously ill. His personality changed, and his outlook on life shifted. I felt abandoned. I was utterly discouraged and heartbroken. It wasn't just one blow; it was a series of hits that I wish I could have stopped. I felt powerless. If it hadn't been for my family, I probably would have curled up and stayed in my bedroom for the entire journey.

At that time, however, a quote from John Sandford resonated deeply with me, keeping me pushing forward. John was a pioneer in heart healing, whose work alongside his wife Paula in the town of Coeur d'Alene, has inspired many ministries and messages. He was like a father figure to me.

The quote stated: "Transformation holds implicitly that nothing in our lives is ever wasted. The prevenient grace of God is so complete that there is no event in our lives without which we could be better off. Transformation, therefore, confirms that Satan has won no victories whatsoever among the saved. For from the ground plan of creation, even as God's plan turned the lowly Cross into the highest victory, so He has designed every aspect of our seemingly defeated lives for glory."

We can often feel like the enemy, however, has won victories. In those moments of despair and confusion, it's hard to see the whole picture. It's a faith walk, a journey of the heart, to trust in God's character and believe in His goodness above what we see with our eyes. God's heart is to seek and to save the lost, even to the last moments.

From the very beginning, before you even arrived on this earth and were formed in your mother's womb, the Lord knew you. You were in His thoughts, and you were in Him. Even before creation, God had a plan to turn the lonely cross into the ultimate victory. He has designed every aspect of our seemingly defeated lives for glory. So don't hesitate to believe that whatever you're carrying, whatever you are going through, none of it is wasted.

I remember being in the midst of profound loss, unsure how I would ever emerge from it. The devastation felt relentless, as trauma followed trauma and experience piled upon experience, leaving me reeling. During the process, I attended a conference in Boise, where my daughters were in the university. I had flown there to be with them, hoping to find some rest and peace.

During the conference, the minister invited everyone to the altar to pray. My daughters and I went forward together. As the minister walked by me, he paused and said, "You shouldn't even be here. The enemy did not want you coming back." He had no knowledge of what I had been through, yet his words struck a deep chord. As he moved through the crowd, he suddenly turned and walked back and stood in front of me. He took my hands and said, "You weren't meant to be here. You were being kicked down so you would not rise again."

I've always been resilient, able to rise after many challenges in life. But this time, his words resonated with the heaviness I felt; I was unsure if I could rise from this overwhelming despair. I recalled sitting with a friend, one of my pastors, during the early days of the betrayals. She held up two fingers, illustrating how small my current struggles were compared to my calling and future. But at that moment, I couldn't see it.

Yet sometimes, even when we've lost so much, the Lord seeks us out. Despite feeling buried beneath my burdens, I realized that hope and restoration were still possible. The minister continued, "What the enemy has done and gone after in your life, he is going to be sorry. Get ready, because the great turnaround is coming." I wasn't yet ready to believe, but his words started sinking into my heart.

I prayed, "I don't know, God. I need You to show me in a way I cannot make up." It was incredible that He would begin the rescue amid my great sadness. During COVID, I was alone in a large house. My husband was in a special rehab facility, and so much was happening. In the midst of it all, I heard the Lord saying, "Whatever comes out of this is going to be for My glory." It doesn't always look like it to us, does it?

It didn't look like that for me. I felt like I had the arrow aimed at the bullseye of my purpose, and then, before the arrows could meet the mark, circumstances and betrayal caused them to fall to the ground. What I thought was my calling was shattered. The wounds of betrayal lodged in my heart and began to fester. I bet all of you reading this book have experienced loss, betrayals, and your own shortcomings getting in the way of relationships, purpose, and longings.

Those circumstances and betrayals in our hearts, they stay, and they go deep. As a little girl, I had arrows shot at me. Some were words like "You'll never amount to anything" or "You're not beautiful." Statements like "You are" or "You are not" are sent forth to destroy. These accusations get stuck in our hearts and fester. They begin to wrap around lies that we start to believe about ourselves. These lies become a filter and a stronghold. It's like a pair of glasses over our eyes, and we come into agreement with what we see through those lenses.

Lies rooted in shame consist of "I am" or "I am not" statements. If you have listened long enough, believed strongly enough, and owned them deeply enough, they will become a part of your identity. They will fortify themselves in you and can dictate your thoughts, beliefs, actions, and reactions. They are an unholy filter through which all thoughts can pass.

Do any of these statements sound familiar?

- I am bad.

- I am unloved.

- I am abandoned.

- I am not good enough.

- I am unworthy.

- I'm all alone.

During that period of my life, I began to believe some of these damaging lies. The most pervasive one was that I was alone, without a defender, and not worth being protected. These lies grew stronger over time, and I found myself aligning with them more and more. This stronghold was so powerful that it resisted the truth of God's Word, even when others tried to pray for me or speak words of encouragement.

Have you ever found yourself in a situation where you hear someone talk about God's goodness, but you feel like it's true for others and not for you? That is how I felt. It was like a downward spiral into hopelessness. I began to discover that these beliefs contradicted with what God says about me. I knew I needed to get a fresh perspective of who God was in the midst of my great sadness.

It took me some time to realize that these beliefs and emotions stemmed from childhood trauma. I'm grateful for a few close friends who could see through my pain and point out when I was believing a lie. Their support meant everything to me during those challenging times.

Believing the lie and being unwilling to believe He is good and wants the best for us is called spiritual rebellion against God. Spiritual rebellion is resistance or opposition to God's authority and His goodness. It involves rejecting or challenging God's commandments, principles, and the benevolent nature of His will. This form of defiance goes against the recognition of God's sovereignty and His intentions for our well-being.

We may say we "love" God and desire to know Him yet find ourselves in a battle with our minds and hearts where the enemy's lies can sound very convincing. When we are trapped in these false beliefs, it becomes difficult to hear and accept the truth of what God says about us. In these moments, we need each other to provide encouragement and to help guide one another back into the light of who Jesus is.

In the midst of my own battle for truth, I found myself making a judgment against God, thinking, "God, You are not a defender or protector." This belief left me feeling that I had two choices: either protect myself by building a wall around my heart and isolating or repent and change my mind about my judgment of God, aligning with what the Bible says about who He is. It took some time for me to truly believe, but by consistently spending time in His presence and reading the Bible, I slowly began to see who He truly is. His goodness overwhelmed me.

God is inviting us to come into agreement with Him so it can be applied in our lives and our hearts. We are sons and daughters of the Most High. We are the bride, the children of the King, Beloved, righteous, redeemed, and joint heirs, we have so much to be excited about. As we embrace the truth about who we are, we grow and mature in our identity. It's like spending time with a truly good father. Our identity is found in Him, as God declares, "I am your Abba Father." Jesus also tells us, "No one gets to the Father but through me," and promises to reveal the Father to us.

Many people have never experienced the love of an earthly father, but Jesus loves the fatherless. He assures them, "I care for you, and I want you to care for them too." He desires for us to understand what it means to have a Father who is good, kind, and gracious—one who wishes to bless us financially, nurture us spiritually, and help us understand our true selves. By getting to know Him, we come to know ourselves, for we are made in His image.

I realized in this season that my greatest gift was His invitation to come to Him. This meant spending time in His presence through meditation of His word, journaling, and being with others who were His hands and feet. It was by slowly getting to know Him in the midst of my tears in the nighttime. At times I couldn't figure out what was right, what was my responsibility and what was others'. It felt so messy, and I remember saying, "God, I don't know what part of this trauma is my doing and what is others'. "Hurt people hurt people. Healed people heal people." People are a part of our healing so, though we want to, we cannot become hermits to protect ourselves. This is how God created our hearts—to be healed by God—and He sets people up in our lives to bring the restoration.

I learned to cry deeply all the way through it. At the end of it, I heard Jesus' voice talking to me, reassuring me. I needed to tell Him all the things that hurt about what was happening. It was so confusing, and I was feeling so alone and lost. I didn't know how to get out of it, but He was there. I decided not to do it on my own. I went to counseling and received the help needed. I cried out to Jesus to speak to me, to rewrite my story, and He did. He is just that good.

Another part of that experience with my daughters that night was the dream I had after the pastor spoke to me. I found myself in a beautiful green meadow surrounded by a crowd, with my friends and people I love nearby. As I was talking to a couple, I saw Jesus walking toward us. I told them, "I'm going to walk with Him," and I turned to follow Him. He had a little lamb tagging along with us. As we walked toward a lake, we started a conversation about the journey I had been on.

Suddenly, the lamb ran past Jesus, heading toward the water. As it was running, I ran with it, letting Jesus know I would keep an eye on it. The lamb, without hesitation, ran right into the water. As it splashed around frantically, I raced to its rescue. Jesus came with me and calmly watched me. As I knelt to reach for the lamb, I saw a big hole in the ground within the water. I reached for the lamb, and to my surprise, there were hundreds of adult sheep, just under the surface of the water. As I watched, it looked as though they were all drowned.

I turned to Jesus, my heart pounding, and cried out, "Jesus, there are sheep in the water, and they have drowned." Tears streamed down my face as without thought I began pulling a female sheep out, crying, "Jesus, she is not alive." I laid it on the green grass outside of the water. To my surprise, it began to cough up the water and suddenly started to breathe. I looked at Jesus, my voice shaking, and said, "They are alive." He said, "Rochelle, do you love Me? Feed My sheep."

I understood what He was saying, and it filled me with a sense of His love and value for the sheep. I said, "I'll do that." However, when I woke up, the reality of my situation hit me, and I wasn't yet ready to hope or believe. I prayed, "Give the dream to me again if it's You." My brokenness was dictating what I believed rather than what God said. I didn't believe God wanted to do anything with me. As far as I was concerned, I was finished, and it was all over.

I fell back asleep in the early hours of the morning, and during those hours, He kept repeating the words over and over to me: "Do you love Me? Feed My sheep." When I woke up the second time, I felt an incredible sense of peace and purpose. I knew that Jesus was with me, guiding me, and that He wanted me to share my journey with others. That dream was a turning point for me. It reminded me that even in the midst of our deepest pain, Jesus is there, offering comfort, healing, and a purpose that goes beyond our understanding.

In response, I began to write. I poured out my heart on digital paper, sharing my struggles, my doubts, and my encounters with God's love and grace. It wasn't an easy process, but it was healing. As I wrote, I could see how God had been working in my life, even in the darkest of times. He had been faithful, and His love had been constant.

I learned to believe that we are never alone. God places people in our lives to help us, to walk with us, and to remind us of His love. And He Himself is always with us, guiding us and giving us the strength to heal and to grow. If you find yourself in a place of pain or confusion, remember that God is with you. Call out to Him, be real with Him, and let Him speak to your heart. Surround yourself with people who can support you and help you heal. And never forget that your story matters. Your journey can bring hope and healing to others, just as God has planned.

We all can believe the lies inserted through some of our greatest traumas as little children. Then, as, we grow up, we often move past the decisions we've made and forget all about them. That's what happened to me with the lie I believed—that I wasn't worth being defended. I thought I wasn't worth it, or I was too much. As an adult, however, I can make those choices to go after the lie and find out where it got hooked. I am able to repent of it, turn toward God, and let Him heal me. Someone else's pain or actions might have affected the decision I made, but I want my heart to be aligned with what the Creator says about who I am so I can live in all of my purpose, on purpose.

The revelation of this lie, for me, came through the healing process. As I was sitting with my prayer minister, she asked, "Rochelle, when did you begin to believe you didn't have a defender?" As we invited the Holy Spirit to reveal the earliest memory, a vision opened in my mind's eye of being in utero. I saw myself just born and laid in an incubator, all alone. It was quiet, with lights above me, and my parents were not present. I wondered, "How could this be real? How could people not know I was born?" I was a twin, but my twin was not with me. The vision felt so real, and I could feel the emotions and sensations of that little infant. I felt set aside, alone, and unworthy. In the midst of those emotions, I concluded that there was no protection for me and that I would have to protect my heart. I vowed to defend myself, feeling unloved and unworthy of protection.

In that moment, I had to reflect on the belief systems I had formed. I judged that God wouldn't be there for me, nor would my parents. This belief made me distrustful, deciding that God doesn't defend when bad things happen or when you feel vulnerable. I began to pray as I sat in the prayer chair with my counselor, "God, forgive me for judging You as unfaithful and for deciding that life would not be safe for me. Forgive me for protecting my own heart and believing lies. I want to come out of the belief that I am unworthy and that no one will be there for me. I want to agree with what You say and forgive those who tempted me to believe otherwise."

As I came out of agreement with the lies, I asked, "What do you say about me?" God responded with a beautiful message: "Even though circumstances made it seem like you were not rejoiced over when you were born, I announced your birth to the heavens. I was excited about your birth." Hearing this deep in my heart made me tear up, and for the first time in a while, I began to believe again that He saw me, knew me, and cared about my life.

I revisited my birth story with my mom, and it confirmed my vision. I was born in Germany, and at that time, mothers were put to sleep during childbirth. She confirmed that she was under anesthesia when I was born and didn't see me for over seven hours. Because I was a small twin, I was placed in an incubator and remained there until the afternoon. I was amazed at how the Holy Spirit revealed that to me.

Telling your story, rather than pushing it down and closing it off, is crucial because it reveals what your heart came to believe. As you share your story, you can uncover which beliefs don't align with the Word of God and what He says about you. God's truth is for you too.

I began to ask the Lord for forgiveness, and He removed the festering arrows of lies from my heart. He reassured me that even though my mother wasn't awake to announce or bless my birth, He celebrated it. He announced my birth to all of Heaven. It takes courage to confront these lies and return to what Jesus says about us. The enemy may try to convince you that you are not valuable, shooting arrows into your heart in such a way that you don't even realize it's there. God's truth brings healing. He has known you and cherished you since you were in your mother's womb.

His thoughts for you are good, even when the enemy tries to destroy you with lies.

Walking this path requires bravery. You may need to revisit and confront painful stories, but this process leads to freedom. It's not about religious or behavioral change, but about a relationship with Jesus. He will guide you gently, and as you come out of agreements with the ways you have judged situations, the ways you have decided to protect yourself, and lies you have believed, you will see yourself in the light of true freedom. We are mountain movers and together, we will find and embrace this freedom. We are called to be a light to our world. We can't do that unless we begin with change for ourselves. We are the light for our families. It starts with us.

You might be saying, "I've been working so hard to get free. It's so painful." That is true, it is incredibly painful at times. However, we are not alone, and we are building a community here at *She Moves Mountains* to be able to walk through this journey faithfully together. I'm inviting each one of you: don't go into denial. Don't just excuse the behavior and say it's your personality. Pursue healing. It's all about relationship—every piece of it and everything you do. Know that God is constantly celebrating you. You are an incredible gift, not just to each other, but to God. I've seen this so many times: the spiritual anointing rises in the room when we honor who God made each of us to be.

As we conclude this chapter, we've seen how the arrows in our lives—both the wounds inflicted by past hurts and the purposeful aims of our dreams and goals—have brought us to a place where God pierces our hearts with His truth. These arrows, once festering with lies and pain, are transformed by His grace into instruments of healing and growth. By confronting our past traumas and aligning our beliefs with God's Word, we find true freedom and embrace our identity in Christ. This journey of healing allows us to use our stories to help others, offering hope and encouragement to those who are struggling. In sharing our experiences, we become vessels of God's love and truth, guiding others toward the same healing and purpose we have found.

Take some time to write in your journal.
Reflect on a time when you felt your purpose was clear. How did that align with God's plan for you?
What pain or betrayal do you need to surrender to Jesus for healing?
How can you use your past experiences to help guide others?

Prayer

Dear Lord, we pray for Your covering. Let these stories begin to saturate us, as the message begins to saturate our souls. Holy Spirit, could it be possible that You think much more highly of us than we do of ourselves? Could it be possible that You have much more that You believe about us, want to see us accomplish, and want to bless us with—financially, spiritually, emotionally, and physically? Jesus, we invite You to come and help us. As this week goes on, help us to take it out, look at it, ask the questions, and discover where we get stuck and where our beliefs are not aligning with Your Word about who we are.

We invite You, Lord, to pour drops of transformation into the hungry hearts of Your people. Stir within us a desire for change and renewal. Set us apart, Lord. May Your Spirit move among us, revealing Jesus in our midst. We ask for Your presence to fill our hearts, in Jesus' name. Amen.

THE SILENT STRUGGLE

Faith is the strength by which a shattered world shall emerge into the light."—Helen Keller

Chapter Six: The Silent Struggle

In the quiet moments of our lives, we often grapple with the silent struggle to truly believe in God's presence and His profound desire to be in a relationship with us. This chapter invites you to examine where your faith currently stands and to explore how it can grow and deepen. You will discover that God not only desires to be close to you but also has a unique and purposeful plan for your life.

Through the transformative power of His Word and Spirit, you are called to align your inner self with what God says about you and who He is. By embracing this transformation, you can move beyond doubt and fear, stepping into a life of faith that reflects the truth of God's promises and the incredible potential He has placed within you. This chapter encourages you to open your heart to the profound relationship God offers—a relationship that empowers you to grow, to believe, and to become all that He has destined you to be.

Our journey of faith is marked by the incredible potential to see the impossible become reality. Jesus teaches us that faith, even as small as a mustard seed, can move mountains and transform our lives in unimaginable ways. This kind of faith requires trust and patience in what we cannot yet see—a hope that compels us to rely on the Holy Spirit to guide and strengthen us through our weaknesses. In our most vulnerable moments, when we don't know what to pray for, the Spirit intercedes with profound emotions, aligning our desires with God's will. This divine partnership assures us that every aspect of our lives is intricately woven into God's perfect plan. With faith, we embrace the potential to see mountains move and experience the fulfillment of God's promises in our lives.

When I was a little girl, I had a favorite tree I would climb, perched high on a mountain amidst the dense woods. I believe it was a pine tree, standing majestically at 60 feet. With childlike enthusiasm and ignorant of the dangers, I would ascend as high as my small arms could carry me, almost touching the sky. To my young heart, that tree was a sanctuary; it felt safe, cradling me within its sturdy limbs, oblivious to the peril each climb potentially held.

Back then, I didn't understand the concept of safety or wisdom; the tree was simply my retreat, a place where faith unknowingly took root in me. Each ascent was more than just a climb; it was an act of faith, a step into the unknown. Without realizing it, I was nurturing a deep-seated faith, a belief in something greater that was forming within me, much like a birth.

As I climbed, I would often lose myself in thoughts of God—pondering who He was, what He meant to my young heart. Even as a little girl, amidst the branches of that towering pine, I felt a profound connection to God, an encounter that seemed as natural as the forest around me.

From that tree, the seeds that were planted on the earth remind us of the beauty that originated in the Garden of Eden. God Himself planted this garden and placed man within it, initiating the beauty we continue to witness across the earth. Every time God spoke during creation, He released a sound, His words echoing through the cosmos. As described in the Scriptures,[1] "So also will be the word that I speak; it does not return to me unfulfilled. My word performs my purpose and fulfills the mission I sent it out to accomplish." These words did not return void but fulfilled the purpose for which they were sent, nurturing life and beauty from the soil of that first sacred garden.

Every time He speaks, He invites us to receive His living Word within us. As we embrace His life-giving Word, He gifts us with the faith needed to believe it. Yet, the challenge arises because the messages we hear around us and the expectations placed upon us may not align with God's intentions. Learning to quiet our souls and organize our thoughts is crucial, especially when fear and anxiety surge in overwhelmingly, leaving us feeling as though we're dodging bullets without a moment's respite. Taking time to understand what's happening within us and deciding how to respond before any given situation is vital. Knowing what voice we will listen to ahead of time is not just helpful—it's essential.

Over the past few years, I've found myself in situations where challenges came at me so swiftly that I needed a strategy in place to prioritize listening to God and His Word first. I would often ask myself, "What will I do when the struggle comes from both within and without?" I wanted to choose to listen to the Word and read the Bible. This practice helps me recognize when circumstances don't align with who Jesus says I am and what my destiny and God's plan are for my life. In every situation, God's Word and who He says I am trumps everything.

God declared that before the foundations of the earth were laid, He knew us. His Word transcends every curse, every harsh word, and every negative comment we have ever heard. Indeed, God's Word overcomes all, but it requires us to step into faith and believe that.

I've sat across the prayer chair from many, listening to their stories and supporting their battles. I refer to these moments as "prayer chairs"—times when we come together to seek God's guidance for both you and me. As we sit together and commune with the Holy Spirit, we often discover that what we believed was false. Together, through prayer and repentance, we step away from the lie and invite Jesus to speak the truth into our hearts.

Through *She Moves Mountains*, you have heard and will continue to learn, lesson after lesson, how to break agreements and realign yourself apart from things that were never meant for you—things that don't align with your created purpose. To me, that's incredibly exciting. In the prayer chair, I've heard countless stories of destinies derailed—stories shaped by lies, fears, trauma, and the distorted views we have through our own lenses. God is inviting us to remove these glasses and embrace the message He proclaimed about us before the foundations of the earth. This truth is far more significant and overrides everything else that has been spoken over you.

When God began the work of creation, as previously noted, He spoke, and immediately light burst into existence. This was before the sun, moon, and stars adorned the sky on the fourth day. Imagine the profound energy and warmth emanating from the presence of the Most High Himself—such was the environment as the firmament took shape and the earth was covered with vegetation.

By the fifth day, God had filled the skies and seas with birds and sea creatures. Yet, it was on the sixth day that something even more remarkable occurred—He created mankind.[2] "Then the Lord God formed the man of dust from the ground and breathed into his nostrils the breath of life, and the man became a living creature." This divine breath is still a part of us today; those who are expecting a child carry within them a new life infused with this same sacred breath, weaving a future filled with destiny.

The creation story continues[3] "And the Lord God planted a garden in Eden, in the east, and there he put the man whom he had formed. And out of the ground the Lord God made to spring up every tree that is pleasant to the sight and good for food, the tree of life in the midst of the garden, and the tree of the knowledge of good and evil." Here, God shaped the earth like a farmer, crafting from it a habitat rich with every necessary provision. From Adam, Eve was formed, continuing the cycle of life that every human being is a part of, regardless of their beliefs or background.

This creation narrative accentuates that each person, at some point, experiences the presence of God, which is essential for life itself. It's in every breath we take, knitted into our being from conception. God invites us to embrace His dream, offering us everything we need for life and urging us to reject the discordant voices that vie for our attention. This is the essence of our existence—continuously encountering God as He breathes life into our purpose.

There are, however, obstacles in our path, and it's worth discussing some of these challenges, as Jesus highlighted them in His teachings. He explained that what is meant to be a steppingstone can become a stumbling block for those who do not know Him. According to the ESV Bible, Jesus came to be the chief cornerstone, the foundation on which we align every aspect of our lives,[4] demonstrating that with such a cornerstone in place, everything else can be constructed perfectly plumb, ensuring a straight and true structure.

Jesus serves as our plumb line, and He has bestowed upon us the Holy Spirit to lead us into all truth, to counsel, and to guide us.[5] However, despite this divine guidance, we still face many challenges in this season.

Like a whirlwind, fear can sweep through our lives, latching onto things of which we haven't let go. Honestly, one of my greatest fears is spiders. I remember vividly when I had to confront this fear. Once, with my son Jonah in my arms, I encountered a spider on the floor. Previously, as a younger person, I had seen a spider crawling on my bedroom wall, and I had reacted by running full speed across our spacious ranch house. In my terror, I ran straight into a large sliding glass door. Luckily, I had not knocked myself out. But, when faced with a spider while holding my child, my protective instinct took over; the spider, unfortunately for it, did not survive. I might have even exclaimed, "In the name of Jesus!" as I dealt with it. While we're called to care for all creatures,[6] sometimes fear overwhelms us and we do what is necessary to resolve the situation quickly.

Fear grips us in many forms, and the spirit of fear operating around us today is palpable. Yet, Scripture reminds us,[7] "For God gave us a spirit not of fear but of power and love and self-control." God invites us out of this captivity of fear, urging us to align with His Word and promises rather than succumb to our fears. This alignment with God's Word empowers us to overcome fears and step out of captivity into freedom.

Another significant issue is the foundational lies we believe, those damaging "I am" statements: *I am unlovable, I am not worth it, I am not seen, I am ugly, I am ignorant, I am stupid, or I am not beautiful*. These statements can trap us in falsehoods. When we believe and partner with these lies, we must approach what I call the well-worn pathway to the cross. There, in a session, sitting across from someone who asks the right questions, we find a beautiful opportunity to confront these beliefs. It's a space where we are invited to examine what we have come to believe and challenge the lies that have taken root in our lives.

What did your heart come to believe in this situation?

When we reject the lies and make room for the truth, we embark on the well-worn pathway to the cross, where Jesus' sacrifice fulfills all requirements. There, we are invited to lay down our burdens, creating space for Jesus to reveal His truth to us. When He speaks, it is profoundly personal. I have witnessed and celebrated God's voice in the hearts of many. He often recalls specific memories, saying things like, "Do you remember when I was there with you when you were four?" Such moments are intimate and personal, shared only with those He deeply loves.

People often break into tears while sitting in the prayer chair, deeply moved by a God who desires to encounter them, speak to them, and tell them the truth about who they are, replacing those lies. This experience is profoundly beautiful and leaves lasting imprints on our hearts. The Bible assures us that God's truths are engraved on our hearts so deeply that we will never stray from believing them again.[8]

Shame (which we'll discuss at length in the next chapter) often acts as a barrier, tightly wrapping itself around us. We hold back from sharing our true stories, haunted by thoughts like, "If they knew the real me, they wouldn't love me." Yet, the truth is quite the opposite. When we embrace vulnerability and open up to people we trust—those who love their Creator and live out that love—we find not only support but also the deep affection for which we yearn.

Many obstacles can hinder this process of opening up. God yearns to lift us out of these confinements. Every day we face the challenge of setting strategies in motion for overcoming these struggles: determining what fears to let go of and whether or not to trust that God's promises are for us too—or even if He exists at all. I relish those moments when people question God's reality because it opens a door. I encourage them to ask God to reveal Himself. God is open to this dialogue; He invites us to seek Him out, promising to respond and make His presence known.

God encountered us at the moment of our birth and is eager to encounter us again. Often, when we turn to Him, it's as if a veil covers our eyes, blocking our ability to see, hear, and spiritually discern. However, when we begin to reach out to the Creator—whether we know Him well, are just beginning to know Him, or haven't yet discerned His presence—all the obstacles in our way begin to dissolve. The moment we say, "Would you reveal Yourself?" He is right there, knocking on the door of our heart. This mirrors the promise:[9] "Behold, I stand at the door and continually knock. If anyone hears My voice and opens the door, I will come in and dine with him, and he with Me." He is ready to lift the veil the instant we invite Him in.

I love that whenever a person turns to the Lord, the veil is taken away.[10] However, a spiritual man does not accept the things of the Spirit of God, for they are foolishness to him, and he cannot understand them because they are spiritually appraised.[11] This illustrates our ability to speak prophetically to ourselves and others as believers. It's like when you're with a friend or spouse over the years, and you recognize the consistency in their character so well that you could refute any contrary claims in a court of law.

This depth of relationship allows us to discern truths about God's character; we know what He would never do because of who He is. When rumors fly about someone we deeply know, we can confidently disagree because our experience tells us otherwise. Similarly, our relationship with God deepens over time, providing us with knowledge of His steadfast nature. Sometimes, when fear or uncertainty overwhelms us, it's crucial to pause and invite the Holy Spirit to be present. I tell myself, "Soul, sit back for a minute. Let's not rush into reacting. Let's hear what the Spirit has to say."

By aligning our spirit with the Holy Spirit, who leads us in truth, we find that many fears and lies directed at us don't hold up because we know who God is—faithful, always there, compassionate, and caring. I've written these traits down because they're so up-lifting.

God is with you and for you. He is always aware of you. He loves who you are now and who you will become, without variance. He doesn't change His feelings based on our progress; He's crazy about us. It's encouraging to realize that you're doing much better than you think. God sees your life from the beginning to the end, from Alpha to Omega. He is in love with you, dedicated to building you up, growing you, and providing what you need to succeed. When we truly know who He is, we can believe what He says about us, even when we face obstacles or attacks in the very areas we were created to excel and expand into the destiny God has placed within us. Take a moment right now to embrace that truth.

[*I pray, Lord, that everyone reading this book would begin to sense the Holy Spirit's destiny for them. May they start to grasp that they were destined for a purpose and a design and may this realization trump everything spoken over them up to now.*]

Growth requires trials, and challenges will come, but the Lord will show us how to navigate through them. He will guide us and change our hearts. Each time He changes us, He does so with the utmost love, helping us to become everything we were meant to be. It is essential we can clearly hear His voice during this process.

God speaks to us in so many ways; He speaks through the Holy Spirit, who reveals Jesus, who reveals the Father. They are three yet one, and we are united with them—a part of the destiny and the plan. As we read in Romans 8, we are a part of that great, vast family. We also hear God's voice through the Scriptures, which become alive and active within us—it's the most amazing message. I've read the Bible numerous times, and each time, it's as if I am gleaning fresh nourishment from the ground, just like Jesus did for Adam and then Eve. I love that.

God also speaks to us through others, whether it's someone preaching with anointing or through this book. Hopefully, you will pick up pieces now and return to gather new pieces, new designs, and new understandings. Revelation and inspiration are going to saturate and transform, because this is the message of God. He doesn't push us to transform because He loves us more for it, but because He wants to help us move into our design and our destiny. As each one of us does that, we will find ourselves partnering with each other in our design and destiny. I don't have to become what someone else is; I can be who I was meant to be.

As well, we hear God's voice in songs, especially during praise and worship. Surprisingly, I've even gleaned messages from movies that aren't overtly Christian—secular films where you wouldn't expect to find a spiritual thread. Yet, something in those movies will strike a chord, inspiring a specific action or decision that remarkably aligns with my destiny. These unexpected revelations become pivotal pieces of my life's journey.

We witness it unfolding in everyday moments, like driving down the street and noticing a message on a license plate that seems to speak directly to us. I often feel this is God communicating with me. To hear Him more clearly, we are invited to seek healing for our wounded hearts, enhancing our ability to discern His messages in the world around us.

As you continue to engage with *She Moves Mountains* over the coming weeks, you'll find yourself eager to learn how to heal your wounded heart. Each lesson is designed to guide you along a path leading to the cross, to the sacrificial love and blood of Jesus. Reflect on the message from Genesis 4:10, where it says the blood of Abel cried out from the ground for justice, and God responded. Just as there has been bloodshed over our nations demanding justice, so too has it been with Jesus. But unlike Abel's blood, which cried for vengeance, the blood of Jesus, as stated in the Scriptures,[12] "speaks a better word than the blood of Abel." It satisfies all divine requirements, offering redemption and peace, truly transforming justice with mercy and grace.

God is compelled to act justly, but instead of directing this justice toward us, He laid it upon Jesus at the cross. Jesus took on what was rightfully ours, allowing us to live as if we had never sinned—justified, as if it never had happened. Handing our burdens over to Jesus is far easier than holding on to our shame, pain, guilt, and the burdens of lies and judgment. Walking this pathway to the cross ushers us into resurrection life, a life filled with abundance that we are invited to embrace.

It's crucial for us to traverse this path, allowing Jesus to speak into our lives once we let go of the obstacles that have bound us. As we release these burdens, Jesus is compelled to act, calling us out and forward into a space of freedom and new beginnings. Would you let Him speak? He wants to lead us into a life of resurrection, where we experience liberty and profound transformation—a life that transcends our past limitations.

He wants you to know Him, to feel alive and well, and to be a change-maker in history. Building strong, heartfelt relationships within our communities, especially in our churches, is crucial for the fulfillment of this mandate. Many of us are seeking deeper connections, reminiscent of the early church described in Acts 2, where believers gathered in homes, shared everything, and had deep fellowship. The Lord invites us to build these relationships—to eat together, share our lives, and engage in conversations that sharpen us, as iron sharpens iron.

In this process of transformation, how can we be sure that our beliefs are truly from God? We can use three guiding principles:

1. Does it align with Scripture? Our beliefs must be grounded in the Bible, which God has given us as a map for our journey. If something doesn't align, it's crucial to return to Scripture and correct our course.

2. Does this resonate with your spirit and the Holy Spirit within you? We are temples of the Holy Spirit, who dwells within us, enriching and strengthening our spirit. If there's unease or a lack of peace, it's a sign to pause and seek where peace and truth reside, often found in patient waiting.

3. What is the feedback from trusted advisors? It's beneficial to discuss our thoughts and feelings with a multitude of like-hearted counselors who share our faith and trust in God. Engaging in dialogue with them can help clarify God's direction, as they offer insights into understanding God's heart and our own spiritual path.

Through these measures, we can foster deep relationships, discern the truth, and navigate our spiritual journeys with confidence and peace.

As we reach the end of this chapter, it's clear that the silent struggle of faith is not just about overcoming doubt, but about embracing the profound truth that God desires an intimate relationship with each of us. This journey is one of continual growth, where our inner selves are transformed by aligning with God's Word and His truth.

We are called to build each other up and strengthen our most holy faith. Here's the distinction: Faith comes from God, and our role is to believe. What we believe determines how we live our lives. We are invited to live according to what God says, rather than being swayed by conflicting emotions or external voices. "Faith is God's part; believing is our part." Let's embrace this, trusting more in God's Word than in our fleeting feelings or the noise around us.

The challenges and uncertainties you face are opportunities for God to reveal His purpose and power in your life. By allowing your faith to deepen and your heart to open, you create space for God to move mightily in ways you never imagined. Remember, you are not alone in this journey—God is with you, guiding you, and shaping you into the person He created you to be.

As you continue forward, hold fast to the truth that your life has purpose and meaning beyond what you can see. Trust in God's plan, allow His Spirit to strengthen you, and watch as your faith transforms your life, enabling you to walk in the fullness of all He has destined for you.

Take some time to write in your journal.
1. *What lies have you believed about yourself, others, or God?*
2. *How does knowing God's truth combat the lies?*
3. *Reflect on a time when God's truth brought freedom in your*

OUT OF THE SHADOWLANDS

"*There is no pit so deep that God's love is not deeper still.*"—Corrie Ten Boom

Chapter Seven: Out of the Shadowlands

In this chapter we start on a courageous journey of battling the giants of shame and moving the mountains of fear and doubt that have long held us captive. Shame, a formidable giant rooted in trauma and painful experiences, distorts our sense of self-worth and creates barriers between us and those we love, including God. Shame can tempt us to believe we are flawed and unworthy, leading to this disconnection in our relationships with others, ourselves, and God. It can even keep us from seeking the help we need as we stay in denial and passivity. Shame can cover us, keeping us captive to self-hatred and self-loathing, making us believe we deserve the shame as a form of punishment.

Through powerful personal stories and spiritual insights, we explore the path to confronting and overcoming these giants by embracing vulnerability and faith. As we learn to trust in God's promises and let go of the past, we find the strength to move mountains that once seemed insurmountable. This journey leads us out of the shadowlands of shame and reveals hidden gifts which empower us to live a life of purpose, freedom, and fulfillment.

When I was little, I loved a pink blanket with silky edges. It was my constant source of comfort and security. One day, the Lord revealed to me that my trauma was like that blanket, wrapping itself around me, securing me in, and hiding me from others. It gave me an excuse to stay in my shame and pain because I believed I deserved it. But God wanted me to see my life and purpose differently, to move beyond dwelling in shame and hiding.

As I became a young woman, the weight of childhood abuse caught up to me and overloaded my emotional circuits. I was plunged into a place of deep sorrow. In the midst of this, my husband's affairs came to light, adding shock and denial to the existing turmoil. The denial was abruptly severed one quiet evening, when my children and I returned from an event and were greeted by the sight of his starkly empty closet—his final departure. We huddled together, enveloped by a poignant silence, our tears mingling with a deep sense of loss and shame. My mind was flooded with the "shame" story—how would this impact our ministry and those we serve? Had I failed God? Was there something inherently wrong with me?

We had already suffered too much—endured ridicule and the physical scars of anger on our walls. Determination rose up in me and I pledged that this would not be our legacy. Holding my children close, I realized it was time to take a stand; the secrets that plagued our home, hidden behind the facade we presented as spiritual leaders, had to end. We were breaking free from the tumultuous, anger-filled life that had raged behind our closed doors.

"I'm sorry it took so long for me to take a stand," I whispered softly as I sat on the couch. I felt the faint vibration of a lion's roar inside me. "You won't have me; you won't have my kids." Committed to a change, I chose to remain in the healing process for myself and learn how to go after healing the broken parts of my heart. I longed for my husband to do the same, but as time went on, our pathways parted. It was devastating, but God was with us, leading us. I made so many mistakes and often, in my own brokenness, missed my kids' hearts.

As I look back, I am so grateful for God's faithfulness and His never-changing grace to heal us and teach us to forgive. Inspired by the promises that God is good, I vowed to go after the healing of our family lines so they might have an easier pathway to walk through their own healing. I would often say, "I may be doing this wrong, but I love you, and I will pay for your counseling if you need it as you get older." I wanted to be the example of freedom out of the shadowlands of shame and out from the bondage of our generational curses.

The brokenness of my life finally drew me into prayer ministry—though it would be a year before I really opened up. I would walk through little bits of my pain at each weekly meeting and began to notice that Jesus always showed up and healed parts of my heart, reconciling me back to Father. He had a sense of knowing what I needed for each part of my heart. Everything I had experienced there in the chair reinforced that God was good and He wanted to heal me. I tentatively began to trust—yet my heart was still so divided. Finally, a prayer minister gave me an ultimatum: "Rochelle, I've taken you as far as I can unless you're willing to start telling your stories."

I had a decision to make: would I fight for my healing or resign myself to staying as I was? During a break of a couple of weeks, I made the decision to contend for healing. When it became nearly unbearable, my counselor would ask me, "What keeps you going? Why are you still here?" My response was a continued echo: "It's for my children and for my children's children. I do not want the things that happened to me to be a curse that continues down the generational line. I'm fighting for them. I'm fighting for me."

I recognized I had been holding back, mostly because I didn't want to defile anyone with the stories. They were so crazy and painful—but I think that was still an excuse. It was my way of staying in denial, mixed in with the fear of being known. The belief in my heart was, "If you really knew me, you might not love me." I had created a presenting facade I let everyone see, like a box: beautiful, ornate and lovely in the ways I thought would make others love me. But deep within, there was another story.

I remember it vividly—the vision of myself sitting by the riverside, feeling as though the Lord had created a fire, just for me, to sit by. It was warm, and the air was filled with misty moisture. I recognized that Jesus was coming down the riverside toward me, and I knew that today was the day I would give Him my box. My heart had come to believe that He was safe.

As He walked closer to me, I found it hard to look Him in the face. But even the slightest glimpse showed me nothing but His love and care for me. He asked, "Are you ready to give Me your box?" I replied, "Yes, I am."

I pulled out of my heart the simple box, creatively designed on the outside, yet so small. I don't even know how all of my stories could've fit in that little box, but I handed it to Him and looked down at the ground, preparing myself for His response. Curiously, I heard Him say, "Oh, did you know that music was in your box?" I looked up slightly and saw Him smiling and holding out His hand, in which rested a small baby grand piano.

In an instant, my memory took me back to my seven-year-old self, sitting in church, pretending to be a piano player. The pianist on the platform had been watching me. After the service, she came down and talked to my parents, inquiring, "Do you know your daughter has the gift of music in her?" That proved to be the first prophetic word I remember over my life, and it began the journey of not only unraveling the stories of pain, shame, and trauma, but of also discovering the beauty of the treasures found within those stories that has formed me into the person I am today.

That vision marked the beginning of my deepest healing. Many of us construct a "box" in which to shove the stories of our lives. The box has beautiful and acceptable outer walls that protect us from the pain and ridicule of others. But shame lives in and around the box and keeps a part of our heart trapped inside with it. These deposited stories of shame, pain, and grief are hidden away, never to be seen again. Since we don't have the Holy Spirit's gift of using a sword that cuts between the marrow and the bone, separating the good from the bad, we scoop up everything—grief, sorrow, and even our good stories—and stuff them into the box. These stories, both painful and beautiful, end up forgotten and left behind as we mature into adulthood.

But Jesus appears and creates a space for us that's warm, inviting, and safe. In this space, we begin to feel safe enough to give our box back to Him. When He opens it, He reveals not only the grief, sorrow, and shame, but also the hidden gifts waiting to be unwrapped. These gifts are the stories that tell us who we are and guide us toward the power of our purpose.

Each one of us has our stories and the proverbial "box" where we have put them away. Some of us have simple wooden boxes, while others have ornate boxes made of different types of metal. We decorate these boxes and present them as though that piece of who we are is all we are. Deep within us, however, is a life ready to be unraveled, healed, and filled with purpose and gifting.

As we walk down the pathway, the Lord lights it so that we can see, experiencing surprises and treasures along the way. These discoveries reveal who we are, who our children are, and who our people are. We uncover newfound gifts we didn't know existed, hidden within the recesses of grief and sorrow, wrapped in the tissue paper of pain. As we unwrap the pain and walk through it, we find that gifts from the Father have been lying on our timeline all along. He holds back nothing to give us good gifts, for every good and perfect gift is from above, coming down from the Father of lights.[1] Looking unto Jesus, the founder and perfecter of our faith, who for the joy that was set before Him endured the cross, despising the shame, and is seated at the right hand of the throne of God.[2]

Walking through this process, it is important we understand the difference between shame and guilt. Guilt is experienced as soon as we sin. It has the power to expose. Guilt surfaces when you do something you know is wrong; however, when you confess it, the Lord is faithful and forgives you from that sin.

But shame is different. It's the problem. Shame does not come from God. It comes from Satan. Shame inspires fear of being exposed, humiliated, rejected, or abandoned.

Shame is the lie we believe about who we are. Guilt says, "I made a mistake," but shame will tell you, "You are the mistake." Because we are so hooked into that lie, shame also keeps us from receiving God's grace. Grace is His undeserved favor; when we feel guilt, we have the privilege of traveling the well-worn pathway to the cross, where we can kneel and admit our behavior is wrong and ask for God's forgiveness.

Shame, on the other hand, will tempt us to believe that we don't deserve forgiveness, keeping us bound to the sinful behavior.

The remedy for guilt is the well-worn pathway to the cross. Jesus has paid the debt for your sin. But the remedy for shame is truth. We need to come out of the belief system we have built around shame, admit it as wrong, and fill our hearts with the Word of God. And we will know the truth, and the truth will set us free.[3] How much more will the blood of Christ, who through the eternal Spirit offered himself without blemish to God, purify our conscience from dead works to serve the living God.[4]

Shame develops when we choose to accept the shame placed on us by others through the demands of performance or unrealistic expectations, and when we are held accountable for things beyond our control. It also comes through words that pronounce a curse over us, like "Shame on you," or "You should be ashamed of yourself." It can also be generated from labels with which people try to define us, such as "You are ugly," "You are stupid," or "You are fat." We begin to believe these labels over what God says about us. It is them we need to remember that the Lord is near to the brokenhearted and saves the crushed in spirit.[5]

We can find ourselves in shame through rejection, abandonment, and neglect. It's important to note that as we're living in relationships by nature, we have needs right from our early years, that not only God, but others, meet for us, like food, shelter, and love. If those needs have not been met and we have experienced neglect and abandonment in our little child heart, we can begin to believe that we are responsible for that—that it's our fault.

We can experience shame through physical or sexual abuse. In shame-based families, strong, painful feelings concerning the abuse are not acknowledged or dealt with, or are hidden under the rug—or not believed. Through this family dysfunction, rigid roles emerge, like the scapegoat, the "hero" the one everybody loves, the substitute mate, or, my go-to, the "good" child. As children, we act out what is expected, and ultimately, this role or performance can be laminated to our personhood, forcing us to forget who we are.

Within its dysfunction, family rules can include: "Don't have feelings," especially ones that rock the boat. In this atmosphere, when a child starts to cry substantially, they are sent to their room to work it out alone, essentially being abandoned.

To complicate matters, burden-bearing, which is a gift from the Lord, can be confusing as you struggle knowing which are your feelings and which are somebody else's feelings in the room. And when you're sensitive, you can be carrying other people's shame—it's not even yours.

Cast all your anxiety on him because he cares for you.[6]

People can also experience shame through the generational line. The Bible acknowledges that curses can affect up to the third and fourth generation,[7] but it also emphasizes that blessings extend to a thousand generations![8]

This biblical truth of shame running through the generational line was more impactful in my own life than I had once known. A few years back, I began to wonder about my history. Where did my parents come from? What was our nationality? It had not been overtly discussed in our family until my mother had passed away about seven years ago in 2017. It was then that all the stories about her Native American heritage began to emerge. At this point, I had decided to delve into an ancestry website to see if I could unravel our lineage. With knowledge of my mother, grandmother, and great-grandmother, I had a foundation to build upon. As I dug deeper, I uncovered that my great-grandmother was born just 30 miles from where I had eventually settled; she was born on the Nez Perce Reservation. What struck me was that, despite all the years I had lived there, she had never shared this detail with me, possibly because of shame.

I recalled my arrival in 1985, when I relocated to this region for a job. One day, I ventured to visit a museum in Spalding, Idaho. As I strolled through the exhibits, the beauty of the handmade canoes and the intricate artifacts captivated me. The faces depicted in the art were stunning. However, as I immersed myself in the stories, a wave of emotion overcame me. I couldn't comprehend how people could be so cruelly treated based on their skin color and the coveting of their land. The tears welled up, and soon, I found myself weeping. The sorrow was so intense that I had to retreat to my car, where I sat and wept, crying out to God, repenting for the injustices committed against these people and their culture.

Many years later, as I discovered that my own grandmother and great-grandmother had lived and attended school on that reservation, the depth of my tears became clearer. They were tears for the pain, the injustice, the sorrow, and the shame of my generations. I realized that, about a hundred years prior, give or take a month or two, my great-grandmother had been born on the very reservation where I stood, moved by the museum's artifacts. I was shedding the tears that my mother, grandmother, and great-grandmother had never been able to shed.

After my mother had passed away, I began to grieve the injustice for her, her previous generations, and for myself. Once again, I found myself sitting in that prayer chair with my prayer minister.

She invited me to talk to God about it. I began to tell Jesus how angry I was that others make the choice to lay you on the altar of sacrifice for their own good. When they're finished with you, they release you and move on as they slowly climb the ladder of success—while leaving so many sacrifices behind them. In my journey as a prayer minister myself, I had heard the stories, I was carrying them, and I was fighting for justice. I was mad at the injustice to people—to women, and to the children—and the injustice in our world.

All the anger I felt was vulnerably shared here in this moment. Not holding anything back, I sensed Jesus asking me to look up. I heard the sound getting louder, "Look up!" As I slowly looked from the left, the past of my generations, to the right, the future of my generations, I knew I was standing in a pivotal moment, calling for justice for all my generations.

Until that moment, I did not realize I was standing right in front of the cross. The sound grew louder; I heard it again, "LOOK UP!" As I looked up, I saw Jesus on the cross, and He said with tears in His eyes, "I chose to go to this cross to be the sacrifice so that you can go free."

I knelt, full of tears of regret for my judgments and relief that He had been there all along. I cried out to my generations, to my mother, to my children, and to my grandchildren, and I said, "Look up, look up! Here is the man who has chosen to be the sacrifice so that we can be free. It's time for us to forgive and repent of our own judgments and the lies we believed so that we can all go free, free from shame."

In this place of tears, of repentance, and of forgiveness, I realized I had sacrificed others on the altar of my own will and my own desires. In the midst of this, I could not only ask for forgiveness but also release forgiveness. My generations, both past and future, could experience the power of the resurrection of life and purpose because of Jesus. This profound realization opened the door to a deeper understanding of how shame works in our lives. Shame can tightly bind our emotions, particularly unresolved and unexpressed feelings such as loneliness, grief, sadness, anger, or jealousy, which can themselves feel shameful.

At times, we might feel shame for having needs, convincing ourselves that we don't deserve love, gifts, or even someone's time. Shame can become ingrained in our identity, especially during childhood. Instead of allowing ourselves to feel anger, for instance, we may be labeled as an "angry child" or perceive ourselves as losers when we experience loss.

When we learn to repress emotions at inappropriate times, we can inadvertently make a vow not to feel or to share. As we grow older, reversing this can seem challenging, but it's actually quite simple. We can bring these feelings to the cross and ask for the reversal of any curses, committing to sharing our emotions and beliefs. This helps us heal and break free from the strongholds of lies that shame has caused us to believe.

To break free from shame, we must first recognize its symptoms. Symptoms may include fear—fear of authority, fear of vulnerability, or fear of expressing our true selves, leading us to wear masks and present a false image to others. We might isolate ourselves to shield from further hurt, find it challenging to have close friendships where we can truly be ourselves, and struggle with self-loathing, often resulting in depression. Engaging in compulsive or addictive behaviors can also be indicative of underlying shame, as can a pervasive feeling of being inherently bad.

To overcome shame, we must be willing to confront it. This begins with admitting the truth about our feelings and actions. Confessing our sins and shame to the Lord and to someone we trust is vital. We must also seek forgiveness and extend forgiveness to those who have wronged us, recognizing that Jesus bore our shame on the Cross so that we could walk in freedom. The Holy Spirit guides us into this truth, helping us to overcome shame's grip on our lives.

It's time for us to decide if we're ready to let the goodness of God break the shame in our lives and allow us to become everything we were meant to be. Others are waiting for us to bring healing and share our stories so they can find freedom. If you're willing, let's begin with this prayer:

Take some time to write in your journal.
  1. *Share an area in your life you have hidden out of shame.*
  2. *Would you be willing to invite Jesus into that place to remove it?*

Prayer for Shame

Behold, I stand at the door and knock. If anyone hears my voice and opens the door, I will come in to him and eat with him, and he with me.[9] Jesus, it's not easy to look at and acknowledge the shameful events of my life, but I want to be healed and free to live the life You have called me to. I choose to open the door to my heart and I invite You into my memory, into the broken places in my heart. I ask that You heal the pain and draw to the cross all shock, trauma, fear, tears, and shame. Gather up the shattered pieces of my heart and make me whole again.

Please cleanse me from disappointment, confusion, and shame, and set me free. I receive Your comfort in the place where I have refused and have been unable to receive comfort in the past.

Sometimes I have felt like David's daughter, Tamar, when she asked, "What about me? Where could I get rid of my disgrace?" I felt that there was no place for my shame and the disgrace I felt. But now I know there is a place, and it is on Your cross. I release the shame to You now.

In the place where my heart has been filled with shame, fear, and distress, I ask that You replace it with Your tender mercies and great, abounding love. I ask that You remove my shame and reproach, and restore me to honor and dignity, which is my true inheritance as a child of the Most High God.

Please grant me the gift of faith to believe in Your promises and enable me to step into my destiny, purpose, and all that You have planned for me.

I believe that You are a kind, loving, and gentle God. Thank you, Jesus, for dying on the cross for me and paying the price for my sin and shame. Lord, I confess that I need You, Your love, protection, power, and deliverance. First John 3:8 proclaims that You came to undo the devil's work. I know that the devil's work is to kill, steal, and destroy.

Shame has been a way the enemy has stolen from me and has brought destruction; but You promised to give me life and life in abundance. I choose to receive Your promise of a full life, and I ask that You set me free from the bondage of sin and shame. Enter every area of my heart and spirit. Set me free from the lies I have believed about You, others, life, and myself, and let me know Your truth in my entire being.[11] In Jesus' name, amen.

PATHWAYS TO FREEDOM

"Though you have made me see troubles, many and bitter, you will restore my life again; from the depths of the earth, you will again bring me up."—Psalm 71:20 (NIV)

Chapter Eight: Pathway to Freedom

The road to healing from trauma is often long and winding, marked by moments of despair and flashes of hope. This chapter, "Pathway to Freedom," explores the intricate journey from captivity in pain to transformation through healing. It delves into the profound impact of trauma on our lives and the courageous steps required to break free from its grip. As we walk this path, we discover that freedom is not just the absence of pain but the presence of peace and purpose. By embracing faith and the transformative power of love, we find the strength to confront our deepest fears and rewrite our stories. This chapter invites you to join us on a journey of healing, offering insights and inspiration as we uncover the keys to unlocking a life of freedom and fulfillment. Together, we will explore how faith, forgiveness, and repentance can light the way forward, leading us out of the darkness and into a future filled with hope.

I want to share with you another part of my journey on the path to freedom. A little less than a year ago, my daughter Maddie, Camille, and I experienced a profound trauma, marking our lives in ways we could never have anticipated. We were in a vehicle collision: hit—head-on. We are now in the process of healing—not just the healing of the physical trauma but also that of the emotional impact and all its unspoken ramifications—some quite unexpected. For instance, I now notice things that previously were invisible to my eye—such as how poorly some people drive.

Our accident happened less than half a block from our house. When we stand on our deck, we can see the exact spot it occurred. The trauma of this event has caused specific symptoms, some of which need specialized care to overcome.

I'm not negating the importance of seeking help when I talk about the healing power of the cross. I keep saying this: the blood of Jesus satisfies all requirements. All we need to do is take the well-worn pathway of the cross. When God says in the Bible, "It's a narrow pathway," it really is. Many people try to find healing elsewhere, and while there exists great healing methods, many necessary, we've learned that the ultimate healing comes from Jesus and the cross.

Jesus, in His love and compassion for us, wants to meet us at the cross. We just need to find that pathway—and girls, you've been finding that pathway as you have walked this journey together. I speak this from experience, as my life has carried me on this very journey. When my kids were young, I went through a significant trauma—the loss of my first husband. He was unfaithful, and as pastoral leaders, his repeated infidelity was incredibly traumatic for me.

But one day, without saying too much, I realized I was strong enough. I had become healthy and had shown up at the prayer chair repeatedly to fight for my healing. I remember sitting across from this beautiful woman who helped me walk through my sorrow, pain, judgment, the vows I had made, and the lies I had come to believe. She helped me rediscover who I was according to who Jesus said I was.

During that process, I remember telling my husband that we couldn't continue like this any longer. It was dangerous. Anger was raging, and everything seemed to turn against me. I didn't know what was right or wrong; I just kept trying to be better and work harder—but I never felt good enough.

He was a beautiful husband—handsome, gifted, and charismatic. He could walk into a place, and people would want to follow him. He had an amazing gift, but the grief was that his heart was broken—he had been broken and abused too.

My children and I had to walk through the process of that loss, and it was a big one. I remember raising my children alone, navigating the trauma of it all. I had told him, "No more, this can't happen like this anymore."

I had hoped he would choose to pursue healing, and that we could heal our marriage together. Trauma is trauma, and its symptoms serve as stark reminders of significant events. He was such a charismatic, talented and capable person, but his brokenness and past abuse were brutal. When he began to confront it, the pain was overwhelming for him. He exploded in agony and said he couldn't do it anymore. Sadly, he walked away and ended up lost in addiction, and near the end of his life, homeless. Trauma affects us deeply, especially from a young age.

Picture an iceberg floating in the ocean, with its tip visible above the water and the larger, hidden mass below. The visible part of the iceberg represents the symptoms of trauma—behaviors and emotions that others might notice, such as anxiety or irritability. However, the true weight of trauma and shame lies just beneath the surface, hidden from view. These deeper emotions are often not immediately apparent to others, yet they profoundly impact how we perceive ourselves and interact with the world. This submerged part of the iceberg is where the most significant and often painful effects of trauma reside, influencing our thoughts and feelings. To heal and move forward, it is essential to address these hidden layers of shame and trauma, acknowledging their presence and working through them to find true freedom and peace.

Trauma is an event outside normal human experience that is beyond our control. It causes us to feel intense fear, horror, or a sense of helplessness or shame. The way we respond to trauma is different for each person. Our temperaments, personalities, and the amount of trauma we've experienced can influence how we respond. Something that may seem small to one person can be very significant to another. It's important to respond with listening and to say, "Thank you for sharing your story with me."

The emotional impact of trauma can manifest as fear and anxiety. The signs can include panic attacks, constant worrying, and ruminating over things. For example, you might say something in a group and then spend days thinking, "That was stupid, why did I say that?" This ruminating is a result of trauma or shame. Other signs can include hyper-alertness or hyper-vigilance. When I was a little girl, I was hyper-vigilant because of the major abuse I had experienced. Until I was 39 years old, I slept with a light on beside my bed. That was challenging for me.

As a young person, I also locked my door, afraid someone would come and badly hurt me. Fear and terror gripped my young life and continued into my adult years. It led to feelings of helplessness and being out of control, which increased my need to try to control my environment.

Trauma can manifest as outbursts of anger, rage, or aggressiveness. You may not even know from where it originates—suddenly, it's just ... there. We need to learn to slow down for a minute and ask ourselves, "Where did that come from? What part of my heart was feeling something at that moment?" That's a part of trauma.

Another aspect is emotional numbing or a restricted range of feelings. You might only feel anger—all other emotions suppressed—making you appear to others as angry or rude. They don't see your sorrow, anguish, or anything else because you learned or were taught never to cry. Holding in tears is not healthy for us, mentally or physically. Additionally, trauma in itself has a negative impact on our bodies.

The Bible teaches us about this type of deep sorrow. Note this verse in Psalms: "By the rivers of Babylon, we sat and wept when we remembered Zion." It speaks to the deep emotions of people who had been captured and taken from their home in Jerusalem. They were sitting by the river in Babylon, a place that wasn't their home. They longed for days gone by, remembering the trauma of being forcibly removed from their city.

It would be like us being kidnapped and moved somewhere else, forced to start a new life while longing for the one we remembered. They were crying and continue their lament: "There on the poplars we hung our harps, for there our captors asked us for songs." The very ones who took them into captivity and were abusing them were asking them to sing songs. Their tormentors demanded songs of joy because they didn't recognize the sorrow in their hearts. They demanded an emotion the captives couldn't show: "Sing us one of the songs of Zion!" But how can we sing the songs of the Lord while in a foreign land?[1]

I recognized this scenario from when my kids were young. As a single mom, I saw my children go through the hardest times after the loss of their father. At around 12 or 13 years of age, one of my sons picked up a guitar, and suddenly, he was a prodigy, playing up and down the scales with ease. He could replicate songs from every era, surprising us all during our music sessions.

How did he learn that? He just knew. But I knew when sorrow and trauma were hitting him because suddenly, the music stopped in our home. This mama's heart knew to pray. The moment the music began to play again, I recognized something was healing.

Even as the kids grew older, having lost their father meant they had lost pieces of themselves. It was like they were orphans—without really being orphans. There was the pain and sorrow of that loss. To combat this, I bought a boat. I remember thinking, "Hey, I'll get us a boat. We'll be on the water, and we'll heal. We'll heal together, my kids and I."

And we did it! We have some of the funniest memories because ... well ... I was a little crazy. If you know me, you'd understand. The boat was cool, but it had way more power than I should have had! In that town, it was all about jet boats. You might be able to picture this: my kids hanging on for dear life, screaming, "Mom!" as we zoomed across the water. I might have caused a bit of extra trauma, it's true. But we laugh about it now. Those wild rides, with me at the helm like a maniac, became a part of our healing journey. We bonded over the chaos and the thrill, and it brought us closer in the most unexpected, hilarious ways.

In the same manner healing can manifest in many different ways, so too, can trauma—including difficulty concentrating. Those who experience this understand that it can be incredibly challenging. Struggling with depression, usually linked back to unresolved trauma, is another heartbreaking expression of trauma.

Unaddressed trauma, unresolved trauma—it sticks around, affecting us in ways we might not even realize. It's a silent companion that can influence our mental and emotional well-being, making it crucial to acknowledge and work through these painful experiences.

Imbedded in the experiences of our trauma, we often find shame lurking. When I was a little girl, I was the "good kid." I wanted to love Jesus, follow what I had learned in Sunday school, and honor my parents. This belief system pushed me to turn all the anger inward when my mother hit me.

I'd scold myself, saying things like, "Why didn't you do that better?" and "Why did you mess up again?" while looking in the mirror and hitting myself, inflicting more trauma.

When I married, I responded the way in which I had been trained: "Why aren't you being a better wife? Why aren't you doing what you're supposed to do?" I continued self-blaming, and it was shame born from the bitterness of trauma.

I hadn't realized these were symptoms of trauma. I had low self-esteem and saw no value in myself except when I did things right and well. When the Lord asked me to step down from the throne I had placed myself on and let Him be Lord, it was really difficult. I had been working so hard to be loved and good enough—but I wasn't successful.

And though I love the Lord to this day, loving Him doesn't necessarily make us good, but it does make us loved and helps keep our hearts open to His love. It helps us learn who we are because of Him, as He loves us amid our pain and struggles.

Dealing with trauma, like the one involving my mother, meant learning to love and forgive myself. It also meant realizing I had to forgive her too, despite the hurt she had caused me. She tempted me to hate myself, but she also tempted me not to love and honor her. This cycle of shame and blame affects so many in our families, creating difficulty in relationships and making it hard to connect heart to heart.

When we feel we cannot escape the trauma, what happens to us? We begin to believe the lie that we are the victim; that there's nothing we can do. I remember this vividly. A fog would come over my brain. I wanted to think logically and solve the issues, but the pain overloaded my circuits, and I froze.

I was therefore incredibly grateful to have people in my life who I could talk to about how I was responding to situations and how to handle them better. My mind was in a state of freeze, unable to figure things out on its own due to the trauma I was experiencing. I relied on others to help me think clearly because I couldn't do it myself. Without the Lord healing me, I wouldn't have been able to make it through. These people taught me things I had missed during my growing-up years. They essentially reparented me, and though it was hard and a bit embarrassing at times, I began to mature.

Knowing what I know now, I could see that through the trauma in my life, I had developed bitter root expectancies, such as thinking that all men would be moved by their sexuality, making me feel unsafe and awkward around them. Bitter root expectancies can cause you to believe something so strongly that it becomes a reality. This made me either use it against them, or never let anyone have my heart again. These bitter root expectations made me a magnet for predators.

Through the losses I had endured, I carried an orphan spirit for most of my life, even though I was surrounded by many great friends. I loved people, but sometimes I would forget myself, and other times, I'd get lost in self-pity, thinking only of me. When I walked into a room, I felt like I had to be the center of attention, exaggerating my presence, while secretly feeling like an outsider who never fit in. These extremes toyed with me, making me feel like I couldn't just be myself.

This orphaned feeling can come from trauma, causing us to live as mere survivors instead of over-comers. We barely get through each crisis, each chaos, before being thrown into another, repeating the cycle. Trauma happens, then shame, and we begin to believe negative things about ourselves, sometimes even wishing we weren't alive.

These outcomes don't seem fair, especially when it is others who harmed us. But coming out of denial means facing these truths. We don't have to live there any longer, but we must recognize that this is how the enemy holds us in captivity. To break this cycle, we need to understand who we are because of Jesus.

The Lord invites us to step out of this cycle of trauma. The spiritual truth is found in Zephaniah: "The Lord your God is in your midst, a mighty one who will save; he will rejoice over you with gladness; he will quiet you by his love; he will exult over you with loud singing."[2]

As I grew older and began to understand more, I found that embracing the Lord's truth set my heart free. I started to believe in who Jesus is, rather than who I thought I was. Repentance became a part of my healing, even though it didn't seem fair. It wasn't fair that I had to go through trauma inflicted by others, or that I had to make choices under those circumstances. But in this broken world, we are at war, and the Lord wants to manifest His love in us and through us.

When I began to heal, I discovered the power of music. I received a beautiful Taylor guitar and learned about tuning it to specific frequencies. This guitar became a tool for ministry. I traveled with a ministry called, A Company of Women, leading worship and singing prophetically over people, touching their hearts with the songs the Holy Spirit gave me.

One powerful moment I recall was releasing a song over a lady at a women's ministry time. My friend asked if I could sing over her sister. I agreed, and as I listened, the Lord prompted me to sing a lullaby. I started to sing this gentle, soothing song, making it up as I went along. The Holy Spirit guided me, and I sang about how He saw her when she would go into her children's rooms at night and sing over them. I described how she touched their cheeks and ministered to their hearts, and that God wanted her to know He saw her and was doing the same for her.

As I sang, the woman had begun to cry. She later told me that she had indeed sung to her children in exactly that way, and it was something deeply meaningful to her. The Holy Spirit used that moment to show her that He saw her, loved her, and was present in her life, ministering to her heart just as she had done for her children.

These prophetic songs became a powerful way for God to reach people, confirming things they had already sensed or revealing new truths. It's incredible how the Lord uses our gifts to bring healing and encouragement to others.

Though trauma can trap us in a cycle of pain and negative self-beliefs, making us feel disconnected from God's blessings, the Lord is calling us to break free from these chains. As we trust Him and allow the Holy Spirit to minister to our brokenness, we begin to heal.

The Bible says in James 5:16, "Therefore, confess your sins to one another and pray for one another, that you may be healed. The prayer of a righteous person has great power as it is working." Let's embrace this truth, confess our stories, and pray fervently, trusting that the Lord will bring healing and freedom.

In the journey through trauma and healing, we've learned that the path is neither simple nor straightforward. Our experiences have shown us the depths of our pain—but also the profound capacity for resilience and recovery. Embracing the healing power of faith and the love of Jesus has been a crucial part of our transformation. Reminding us that true healing comes not only from understanding our wounds but also from embracing the hope of redemption. As we continue to navigate the complexities of trauma, let us hold onto the truth that we are not defined by our past but by the love and strength we find in our journey with God. Through shared stories, support, and unwavering faith, we can move forward, healed and whole, ready to embrace the future with renewed hope and purpose.

Take some time to write in your journal.
1. *Reflect on a time when you felt trapped by trauma. How did you begin to Find freedom?*
2. *How are you able to help others on their journey to freedom?*

PRAYERS

"The Lord is close to the broken hearted and saves those who are crushed in spirit"—Psalm 34:18 (NIV)

Before we begin, I invite you to find a quiet and comfortable place where you can fully engage with this prayer. Take a moment to gather a journal and a pen, as you may want to write down any thoughts, reflections, or insights inspired during this time. If you like, wrap yourself in a blanket for warmth and comfort. Whether you choose to sit or lie down, allow yourself to relax and open your heart to what God may reveal to you. As we pray together, I encourage you to expect an encounter with the Holy Spirit, who is here to reveal Jesus to you in a profound way. This is a sacred space where healing and transformation can begin. Trust that you are in a safe place, embraced by the love of God and surrounded by His presence.

Enter his gates with thanksgiving and his courts with praise! Give thanks to him; bless his name[1]

Trauma can hold us back from experiencing the Lord and being grateful. Therefore, let's tune our hearts to gratitude. Take a moment to reflect: What am I thankful for? If you can't think of anything, ask Jesus, "Would You give me something to be thankful for?"

[*Take a moment to write your gratitude in your journal.*]

Let me share my vision with you, as it gives a clear visual of the greatness of the Lord. As I prepared to pray, I envisioned us walking through the gates and into the courts, immediately embraced by the vibrant sounds of a bustling courtyard. A beautiful harmony of praise and thanksgiving fills the air, creating an ecstatic symphony dedicated to the One who holds everything together. This place is vast, capable of hosting thousands upon thousands.

Ahead, way up front, I see Abba Father on His throne. He exudes both a judicial presence and a fatherly warmth. I come before Him in this sacred space to seek healing for my heart and realignment with His purpose for me. The immense size of His throne speaks to His unparalleled authority—the highest of all gods, kings, and thrones.

As I gaze upon the awe of His glory and power, it's overwhelming to stand before Him. I know I can only be here because of the power of Jesus' blood, responding to His invitation to come boldly into the throne room. I know I wouldn't be safe here if it hadn't been for Yeshua Jesus' sacrifice. The blood of Jesus meets all the requirements, and I've come by the blood of the Lamb and the word of my testimony. Walking up the aisle, I notice the many faces on both sides: the great cloud of witnesses cheering me on and those who are my accusers. I know there's an accuser armed with God's laws against me, hands full of my infractions—too many to count. He's been accusing me my whole life, trying to keep me in a twisted understanding of who I am and who God is. Fixing my eyes on Jesus, I take my place beside Him in front of the judicial throne.

Lord, as we pray and make our requests, we know that at this throne, the Bible says, "Righteousness and justice are the foundation of your throne; steadfast love and faithfulness go before you."[2] These foundations are firm and unshakable. There is no moving this throne or changing its rules. Righteousness and justice are immovable foundations, and this is wonderful news. We are deeply grateful for this.

The enemy tries to tether our hearts and move us since he can't move the throne. He tries to make us wonder, "Is that really what God said about me? Is that really who God is?" But we come before You in these courts of heaven with praises and with our advocate, Yeshua, who the Bible says, "always lives to make intercession for us."[3] We're coming into agreement with His truths of righteousness and justice.

As we enter, we recognize the warmth and movement, almost like warm rainbow colors and the sounds of His voice in perfect frequency, right before the throne. The Bible says, "His steadfast love endures forever,"[4] and "His faithfulness reaches to the skies."[5] If I can lean into His steadfast love and His faithfulness, then I know I am right under the shadow and the shelter of His wing. This is where I want to be—in awe of His presence.

Everything that You, Abba Father, think of me in this place under the shadow of the Most High is through the eyes of faithfulness and steadfast love. You know the trauma I've been through, and You are ready to move into action on my behalf. So today, I come before You and ask, would You envelop me in the warmth of Your presence?

After the resurrection, Jesus, Your heartbeat echoed with the rhythm of the Kingdom, beyond the reach of any earthly challenge. There was no more hardship, no more obstacles, and no one trying to harm you. You walked with the men on the road to Emmaus, and they said, "Didn't our hearts burn within us while he talked to us on the road, while he opened to us the Scriptures?"[6] You walked through a locked door to meet with the twelve,[7] and with the simplicity of a phrase, You turned their trauma into hope as You spoke, "Peace be with you." Then, the same, with 500 at one time.[8]

No punishment—whether from human culture, corrupt governments, or religious persecution—could ever truly harm You. You transcended the laws of nature, appearing and disappearing as effortlessly as a whisper. Before Peter even brought the fish in, You had already provided breakfast, surprising him with Your generous provision, and gently inviting him to feed Your sheep.

133

When You spoke Mary's name at the tomb, it was as if the sun broke through the clouds, melting away her fear, trauma, and sorrow. At that moment, the agony of witnessing the death of everything she believed in was dispelled by the tender sound of You speaking her name. Now, all she could feel was the radiant hope of Your resurrection, the promise fulfilled, and the overwhelming love of her Rabbi.

In that sacred place of resurrection, Jesus, where Your voice, so gentle and compassionate, broke through the dawn, asking Mary, "Who are you seeking?" we, too, respond with hearts wide open. We are seeking You to heal our wounds. We yearn for a judge who rules with unshakable justice and righteousness, one who keeps His promises. We ask for the healing You've promised and for dreams yet to unfurl.

Here in this sacred place, I ask You to honor our requests as we humbly repent and forgive. Let the things the enemy has done in our lives be brought to death on the cross so our true lives can be resurrected to abundant life once again. Resurrection looks like something—freedom. The war is beginning to subside as I move into Your presence. In this place, Your righteousness and justice are immovable. Before You swirl the movement of faithfulness and steadfast love, and it will go with me, before me, in me, through me, and accomplish everything You tell it to accomplish.

You see me. You know what I've been through. You know the trauma I've endured, and I believe You are ready to act on my behalf. Lord, we thank You for making it safe for us to pray. Thank You for restraining every force of darkness that would seek to interfere or hinder this healing and for forbidding any harassment, intimidation, or retaliation against us, any part of us, anyone we love, and anything You have given us.

[As we begin to pray, when things come to mind, write them down in your journal.]

Thank You for rebuking the forces of darkness that have sought to harm us or have tried to keep us locked in this prison of trauma. You have not given us a spirit of fear but of love, power, and soundness of mind, and that is what we claim and agree together for today. Thank You for contending with those who are contending with us. Lord Jesus, I invite You to come as the Prince of Peace and bring Your peace to us. Establish Your dominion of peace and manifest Yourself in such a way that we will know You are here. Enable us to feel the depths of Your love.

Jesus, we invite You into this place. Holy Spirit, would You reveal where Jesus is and what He is doing? Lord, would You hide us away under the shadow of Your wings?[9] I break every assignment of trauma against us, and resist and send away every "guard" assigned.

I declare over you the promise of the Lord Jesus Christ: "For I know the plans I have for you, declares the Lord, plans for welfare and not for evil, to give you a future and a hope."[10] Lord Jesus, I ask You to draw all of the pain, trauma, shock, and fear from within us, bringing it all to effective death on the cross. I declare that what is brought to death has no more power to harm or destroy. You suffered and died for us. We appropriate all You accomplished for us on the cross. May Your resurrection power and life flood through us and through our very being right now as we stand here in this place before the Lord. You know what we have been through. You know the pain, the sorrow, the grief, the loss, the fear, and the confusion.

Please take our hand and walk with us down the timeline of our life. Heal every instance of shock, trauma, fear, and dread from the crown of our heads to the soles of our feet. In the name of Jesus, I declare that the power of shame that has kept the traumas hidden and unaddressed is forever broken. We allow You to unwrap us from the shame that has bound us and ask that You fill us with Your glory. Release the revelation of how precious we are to You and how much You love us.

As You pour Your steadfast love, faithfulness, and grace, please remove and draw to the cross any trauma stored in the cells of our bodies. Restore the cells to perfect order, vibration, frequency, function, and design. Please remove any shock, trauma, fear, terror, or shame experienced at conception, in the womb, or during birth. I bless the moment of your conception. I bless the time when you were being knit together in your mother's womb.[11] I bless the moment of your birth and call you forth in the newness of life. You are welcome on this earth. There is a place for you here.

Your heavenly Father desires you to prosper in every single way. I invite you to live, to thrive, and embrace the abundant life Jesus longs to give you. Lord, thank you for healing us in our DNA. Remove every shock, trauma, fear, terror, and shame that has come through the generational flow. We place the cross of Jesus firmly between us and our generations. We ask that all iniquity be stopped at the cross of Christ.[12]

Thank You for forgiving us and those in our generations who traumatized others, who manipulated, dominated, or controlled through fear and torment. We ask You to release Your precious blood and heal all unresolved grief and pain, cleansing us from all unrighteousness.[13] This is a place for forgiveness. Though we may not fully understand how these patterns have developed over time, we recognize their persistent repetition across generations. We invite You, Lord, to heal our generations. We declare that, from this day forward, the landmark of our generation is marked by the cross, the blood of Jesus, and the empty tomb because of His resurrection.

We declare that forgiveness and repentance will radiate from this choice today. We will no longer be traumatized by the choices of past generations, especially those involving Masonic practices, witchcraft, occultism, and all false religions. Today, we proclaim that our generation is now dedicated to You and Your Kingdom. This dedication extends from our ancestors to our children and our children's children.

Heal the "fear center" of our brain and every place where memory is processed and stored. Remove all shock, trauma, fear, terror, and shame from the conscious, unconscious, and subconscious memory, and draw from us all the pain that has caused so much torment. Turn off the alarms that have been ringing for so long, and replace the fear, dread, and hyper-vigilance with godly discernment. Let us know when danger is truly present and give wisdom to know how and when to respond. Bring peace and rest to the part of the heart that has always had to stand guard and be alert; remove any pervasive low-level anxiety.

Thank You for removing the emotional energy that has wrapped around the traumatic memories. Please help us to process the memories so they can be stored not as raw data but as a part of our testimony: a part of our story that no longer has the power to destroy or harm us but begins to be why we can come to this court, why we can stand here. We come because of the blood of the Lamb and the power of our testimony.[14]

I invite you to come into this place of peace and rest in Christ. Jesus, You are a good shepherd. Thank You for filling every area of unmet need with Your love and Your peace according to Your riches in glory.[15] Many times, our needs aren't met in places like this, and we need the language to tell people what we really need. But we recognize that it's missing. Would You release us from the trauma of even people who did not respond in the way we needed? We forgive them. I know how many times I have not responded in the way others required me to respond.

Thank You for healing every father wound, every mother wound. Fill the longing in our hearts for love, comfort, protection, and blessing. Remove every arrow of hurtful, shameful things spoken over us that pierced our hearts. Break the power of every lie we have come to believe and sing over us the truth of who You are and who You created us to be. Heal every wound of rejection and abandonment. Grant an inner knowing that we are accepted and loved, that we are Your children, and You love us with an everlasting love.[16] Establish deep within us the truth that You will never leave us nor forsake us.[17]

Establish new neurological connections to the joy center of the brain, enabling us to have a full range of emotions as You have purposed. Teach us to express our emotions wisely and honorably because we need them, all of them. Heavenly Father, thank You for removing the trauma from our eyes and ears.

I release the precious blood of Jesus to wash away every ungodly, unholy, traumatic image seared upon our soul and spirit. Thank You for removing the trauma from any harmful or harsh words spoken over us. Thank You for removing the trauma associated with scents, smells, and from our skin.

I invite all parts of your body and soul that are holding on to the shock, trauma, fear, terror, and shame to release it now to Jesus Christ. If you choose, say, "I give it to You, Lord. I choose to give it to You. Every part of my heart that's willing, I let it go to You because You're good ... because You're faithful ... because I'm starting to believe You. I want to be restored

138

to my original design and function and come into peace. Heavenly Father, sing Your song over us and bring everything within us into agreement with Your song and original design.[18] Help us hear the song You sing over us. Sing it over us in the night seasons as You say You do. You twirl like a top around us, excited about who we are, full of colors and movement.

Bring our hearts into agreement with Your song and Your original design. In the name and the blood of Jesus Christ, I prophesy order and healing in spirit, soul, and body. Trauma has shaken us to the core of our foundation. In Jesus' name, I release God's love into every crack and crevice in that foundation. Father, restore the ability and grace to trust again, hope again, be willing to live again, receive Your promises, and believe wholeheartedly in You.

Thank You for removing all shock, trauma, fear, terror, and shame from our will and spirit. Restore will and strength in every way. Could You give us back our "yes" and our "no?" Please give us back our choices, not to be a victim any longer, but to be a victor with You beside us. We're going to walk this out because You have every good thought in mind for us. You are faithful.

Thank You for removing all shock, trauma, fear, terror, and shame from the muscles, ligaments, tendons, bones, and bone marrow. Bring Your healing power to every area where we and our spirits have been crushed or broken. Restore health, vitality, and vigor. Make the bones and connective tissues strong again. Thank You for removing all shock, trauma, fear, and terror from the organs.

[Place your hand on any part of your body that needs it and say, "I lift off every shock, trauma, fear, terror, and shame residing here."]

Thank You for healing the immune system and removing all toxins that remain from any chemicals or hormones that have poured through our bodies for so many years. Lord, would You lift off every shock, terror, trauma, fear, and shame that's been wrapped around the stories and hooked to all those places in our bodies? Draw it to the cross because Jesus' blood satisfies all the requirements now.

Here before You, King Jesus, and Abba Father, would You declare over us these things finished? Cancel any and all effects that it's had on our spirit, soul, and body, and restore all neurochemical balance. Thank You for breaking the power of and severing all fear bonds, trauma bonds, and unhealthy and unholy soul ties created through reaction to trauma.

Help us to receive this healing and have the courage to resolve anything that remains unresolved. Help us to recognize and bring to death all the old ways of responding and reacting to shock, trauma, fear, and terror. Reveal any place where we may be stuck in trauma response that has become a practiced way of self-protection. Thank You for empowering us with wisdom and grace to dismantle ungodly structures of defense and rebuild new God-structures based on Your Scriptures, such as discernment, the prophetic, and our free will to say "yes" and "no." Teach us Kingdom ways and victorious ways and help us come to a true understanding of our spiritual authority as children of the Most High.

Thank You for filling every cell in our bodies with Your peace and healing grace, displacing darkness with Your light. Keep us in Your perfect peace, especially in the night seasons, and bring restorative rest. Thank You for forbidding retaliation or backlash against us, any part of us, anyone we love, and anything You have given us. Father God, I ask You to pass judgment on the enemy and set us free. Declare in the justice and righteousness of Your foundation that we are free from this trauma.

Bring us back into perfect alignment with steadfast love and faithfulness. Papa God, kiss Your child as a papa would kiss his beloved child. May Your favor and protection surround us like a shield. Seal this work that You have done, Lord, so that nothing may be lost. In Jesus' name, we pray. Amen.

References for Chapter 1: He Still Moves

1. Matthew 6:9-10 - "Pray then like this: 'Our Father in heaven, hallowed be your name. Your kingdom come, your will be done, on earth as it is in heaven.'"

2. Esther 4:14 - "For if you keep silent at this time, relief and deliverance will rise for the Jews from another place, but you and your father's house will perish. And who knows whether you have not come to the kingdom for such a time as this?"

3. Genesis 1:3-5 - "And God said, 'Let there be light,' and there was light. And God saw that the light was good. And God separated the light from the darkness. God called the light Day, and the darkness he called Night. And there was evening and there was morning, the first day."

4. Genesis 1:6-8 - "And God said, 'Let there be an expanse in the midst of the waters, and let it separate the waters from the waters.' And God made the expanse and separated the waters that were under the expanse from the waters that were above the expanse. And it was so. And God called the expanse Heaven. And there was evening and there was morning, the second day."

5. Genesis 1:9-13 - "And God said, 'Let the waters under the heavens be gathered together into one place, and let the dry land appear.' And it was so. God called the dry land Earth, and the waters that were gathered together he called Seas. And God saw that it was good."

6. Genesis 1:14-19 - "And God said, 'Let there be lights in the expanse of the heavens to separate the day from the night. And let them be for signs and for seasons, and for days and years, and let them be lights in the expanse of the heavens to give light upon the earth.' And it was so."

7. Genesis 1:20-23 - "And God said, 'Let the waters swarm with swarms of living creatures, and let birds fly above the earth across the expanse of the heavens.' So God created the great sea creatures and every living creature that moves, with which the waters swarm, according to their kinds, and every winged bird according to its kind. And God saw that it was good."

8. Genesis 1:24-26 - "And God said, 'Let the earth bring forth living creatures according to their kinds—livestock and creeping things and beasts of the earth according to their kinds.' And it was so."

9. Genesis 1:27-28 - "So God created man in his own image, in the image of God he created him; male and female he created them. And God blessed them."

10. Genesis 2:16-17 - "And the LORD God commanded the man, saying, 'You may surely eat of every tree of the garden, but of the tree of the knowledge of good and evil you shall not eat, for in the day that you eat of it you shall surely die.'"

11. Genesis 3:1-6 - "Now the serpent was more crafty than any other beast of the field that the LORD God had made. He said to the woman, 'Did God actually say, "You shall not eat of any tree in the garden"?'"

12. Genesis 3:7 - "Then the eyes of both were opened, and they knew that they were naked. And they sewed fig leaves together and made themselves loincloths."

13. Genesis 3:8-9 - "And they heard the sound of the LORD God walking in the garden in the cool of the day, and the man and his wife hid themselves from the presence of the LORD God among the trees of the garden."

14. Genesis 3:12-19 - "The man said, 'The woman whom you gave to be with me, she gave me fruit of the tree, and I ate.'"

15. Psalm 147:3 - "He heals the broken-hearted and binds up their wounds."

16. Matthew 11:28 - "Come to me, all who labor and are heavy laden, and I will give you rest."

17. James 5:16 - "Therefore, confess your sins to one another and pray for one another, that you may be healed. The prayer of a righteous person has great power as it is working."

18. Hebrews 9:14 - "How much more will the blood of Christ, who through the eternal Spirit offered himself without blemish to God, purify our conscience from dead works to serve the living God."

19. James 4:7 - "Submit yourselves therefore to God. Resist the devil, and he will flee from you."

20. Jeremiah 29:11 - "For I know the plans I have for you, declares the LORD, plans for welfare and not for evil, to give you a future and a hope."

21. Hebrews 12:24 - "And to Jesus, the mediator of a new covenant, and to the sprinkled blood that speaks a better word than the blood of Abel."

22. Romans 5:9 - "Since, therefore, we have now been justified by his blood, much more shall we be saved by him from the wrath of God."

23. 1 Peter 2:24 - "He himself bore our sins in his body on the tree, that we might die to sin and live to righteousness. By his wounds you have been healed."

24. Matthew 7:13-14 - "Enter by the narrow gate. For the gate is wide and the way is easy that leads to destruction, and those who enter by it are many. For the gate is narrow and the way is hard that leads to life, and those who find it are few."

25. Philippians 2:10-11 - "So that at the name of Jesus every knee should bow, in heaven and on earth and under the earth, and every tongue confess that Jesus Christ is Lord, to the glory of God the Father."

26. Acts 14:15 - "'Men, why are you doing these things? We also are men, of like nature with you, and we bring you good news, that you should turn from these vain things to a living God, who made the heaven and the earth and the sea and all that is in them.'"

27. John 5:19-20, 30 - "So Jesus said to them, 'Truly, truly, I say to you, the Son can do nothing of his own accord, but only what he sees the Father doing. For whatever the Father does, that the Son does likewise.'"

28. John 3:16 - "For God so loved the world, that he gave his only Son, that whoever believes in him should not perish but have eternal life."

29. John 1:11-12 - "He came to his own, and his own people did not receive him. But to all who did receive him, who believed in his name, he gave the right to become children of God."

30. Acts 2:38 - "And Peter said to them, 'Repent and be baptized every one of you in the name of Jesus Christ for the forgiveness of your sins, and you will receive the gift of the Holy Spirit.'"

Additional verses:

- Isaiah 41:10 - "Fear not, for I am with you; be not dismayed, for I am your God; I will strengthen you, I will help you, I will uphold you with my righteous right hand."

- Psalm 23:4 - "Even though I walk through the valley of the shadow of death, I will fear no evil, for you are with me; your rod and your staff, they comfort me."

- Isaiah 40:31 - "But they who wait for the LORD shall renew their strength; they shall mount up with wings like eagles; they shall run and not be weary; they shall walk and not faint."

References for Chapter 2: Presence

1. Psalm 110:1 - "The Lord says to my Lord: 'Sit at my right hand until I make your enemies a footstool for your feet.'"

2. Acts 2:17-18 (ESV) - "'And in the last days it shall be, God declares, that I will pour out my Spirit on all flesh, and your sons and your daughters shall prophesy, and your young men shall see visions, and your old men shall dream dreams; even on my male servants and female servants in those days I will pour out my Spirit, and they shall prophesy.'"

3. Jeremiah 29:11 (ESV) - "'For I know the plans I have for you,' declares the Lord, 'plans for welfare and not for evil, to give you a future and a hope.'"

4. Hebrews 13:8 (ESV) - "Jesus Christ is the same yesterday and today and forever."

5. John 20:19-22 (ESV) - "On the evening of that day, the first day of the week, the doors being locked where the disciples were for fear of the Jews, Jesus came and stood among them and said to them, 'Peace be with you.' When he had said this, he showed them his hands and his side. Then the disciples were glad when they saw the Lord. Jesus said to them again, 'Peace be with you. As the Father has sent me, even so I am sending you.' And when he had said this, he breathed on them and said to them, 'Receive the Holy Spirit.'"

6. Acts 1:4-5 (ESV) - "And while staying with them he ordered them not to depart from Jerusalem, but to wait for the promise of the Father,

which, he said, 'you heard from me; for John baptized with water, but you will be baptized with the Holy Spirit not many days from now.'"

7. John 4:23 (ESV) - "But the hour is coming, and is now here, when the true worshipers will worship the Father in spirit and truth, for the Father is seeking such people to worship him."

8. James 4:10 (ESV) - "Humble yourselves before the Lord, and he will exalt you."

9. 1 Corinthians 13:1 (ESV) - "If I speak in the tongues of men and of angels, but have not love, I am a noisy gong or a clanging cymbal."

Additional verses:

- Matthew 28:20 - "And behold, I am with you always, to the end of the age."

- Psalm 46:10 - "Be still and know that I am God. I will be exalted among the nations; I will be exalted in the earth!"

- 2 Corinthians 3:17 - "Now the Lord is the Spirit, and where the Spirit of the Lord is, there is freedom."

- Romans 8:38-39 - "For I am sure that neither death nor life, nor angels nor rulers, nor things present nor things to come, nor powers, nor height nor depth, nor anything else in all creation, will be able to separate us from the love of God in Christ Jesus our Lord."

- Psalm 139:7-10 - "Where shall I go from your Spirit? Or where shall I flee from your presence? If I ascend to heaven, you are there! If I make my bed in *Sheol*, you are there! If I take the wings of the morning and dwell in the uttermost parts of the sea, even there your hand shall lead me, and your right hand shall hold me."

References for Chapter 3: He Whispers

1. Genesis 1:26 - "Then God said, 'Let us make man in our image, after our likeness. And let them have dominion over the fish of the sea and over the birds of the heavens and over the livestock and over all the earth and over every creeping thing that creeps on the earth.'"

2. Psalm 139:13-14 - "For you formed my inward parts; you knitted me together in my mother's womb. I praise you, for I am fearfully and wonderfully made. Wonderful are your works; my soul knows it very well."

3. 1 Kings 17:1 - "Now Elijah the Tishbite, of Tishbe in Gilead, said to Ahab, 'As the LORD, the God of Israel, lives, before whom I stand, there shall be neither dew nor rain these years, except by my word.'"

4. Psalm 119:105 - "Your word is a lamp to my feet and a light to my path."

5. *Communion with God* course by Mark and Patti Virkler - Refer to this course for guidance on hearing God's voice and maintaining communion with Him. www.CWGministries.org

6. *Four Keys to Hearing God's Voice,* available - This resource provides practical steps for hearing God's voice.

7. Jeremiah 29:13 - "You will seek me and find me, when you seek me with all your heart."

8. Matthew 6:6 - "But when you pray, go into your room and shut the door and pray to your Father who is in secret. And your Father who sees in secret will reward you."

9. Psalm 100:4 - "Enter his gates with thanksgiving, and his courts with praise! Give thanks to him; bless his name!"

10. Matthew 13:35 - "This was to fulfill what was spoken by the prophet: 'I will open my mouth in parables; I will utter what has been hidden since the foundation of the world.'"

11. Mark 4:33-34 - "With many such parables he spoke the word to them, as they were able to hear it. He did not speak to them without a parable, but privately to his own disciples he explained everything."

12. Psalm 23:4 - "Even though I walk through the valley of the shadow of death, I will fear no evil, for you are with me; your rod and your staff, they comfort me."

13. Psalm 23:4 - "Even though I walk through the valley of the shadow of death, I will fear no evil, for you are with me; your rod and your staff, they comfort me."

14. Hebrews 13:5 - "Keep your life free from love of money, and be content with what you have, for he has said, 'I will never leave you nor forsake you.'"

15. Habakkuk 2:2 - "And the LORD answered me: 'Write the vision; make it plain on tablets, so he may run who reads it.'"

16. John Paul Jackson - Refer to John Paul Jackson's teachings for insights on prophetic ministry and hearing from God. https://streamsministries.com/

17. Streams Ministry - A ministry founded by John Paul Jackson, focused on prophetic training and understanding dreams. https://streamsministries.com/

18. Hearing God through your Dreams by Mark Virkler - A resource on understanding and interpreting dreams as a way of hearing from God. www.cwgministries.org/store/hearing-god-through-your-dreams.

19. Dream Encyclopedia by Barbie Breathitt - A comprehensive guide to understanding the symbols and meanings of dreams in a biblical context. https://dreamsdecoder.com

20. Psalm 23:3 - "He restores my soul. He leads me in paths of righteousness for his name's sake."

21. John 10:27 - "My sheep hear my voice, and I know them, and they follow me."

22. John 14:12 - "Truly, truly, I say to you, whoever believes in me will also do the works that I do; and greater works than these will he do, because I am going to the Father."

23. Psalms 119:105 – "Your word is a lamp to my feet and a light to my path."

24. 1 Corinthians 14:5 - "Now I want you all to speak in tongues, but even more to prophesy. The one who prophesies is greater than the one who speaks in tongues, unless someone interprets, so that the church may be built up."

25. 1 Corinthians 14:1 - "Pursue love, and earnestly desire the spiritual gifts, especially that you may prophesy."

26. Hebrews 10:25 - "Not neglecting to meet together, as is the habit of some, but encouraging one another, and all the more as you see the Day drawing near."

27. 1 Kings 17:18 - "And she said to Elijah, 'What have you against me, O man of God? You have come to me to bring my sin to remembrance and to cause the death of my son!'"

28. 1 Kings 17:20 - "And he cried to the LORD, 'O LORD my God, have you brought calamity even upon the widow with whom I sojourn, by killing her son?'"

29. 1 Kings 17:21 - "Then he stretched himself upon the child three times and cried to the LORD, 'O LORD my God, let this child's life come into him again.'"

30. 1 Kings 17:23 - "And Elijah took the child and brought him down from the upper chamber into the house and delivered him to his mother. And Elijah said, 'See, your son lives.'"

31. 1 Kings 17:24 - "And the woman said to Elijah, 'Now I know that you are a man of God, and that the word of the LORD in your mouth is truth.'"

Additional verses:

- Isaiah 30:21 - "And your ears shall hear a word behind you, saying, 'This is the way, walk in it,' when you turn to the right or when you turn to the left."

- John 16:13 - "When the Spirit of truth comes, he will guide you into all the truth, for he will not speak on his own authority, but whatever he hears he will speak, and he will declare to you the things that are to come."

- Proverbs 3:5-6 - "Trust in the LORD with all your heart, and do not lean on your own understanding. In all your ways acknowledge him, and he will make straight your paths."

References for Chapter 4: Tell Her Story

1. Zephaniah 3:17 - "The LORD your God is in your midst, a mighty one who will save; he will rejoice over you with gladness; he will quiet you by his love; he will exult over you with loud singing."

2. Luke 1:37 - "For nothing will be impossible with God."

Additional verses:

- Isaiah 55:11 - "So shall my word be that goes out from my mouth; it shall not return to me empty, but it shall accomplish that which I purpose, and shall succeed in the thing for which I sent it."

- Psalm 68:11 - "The Lord gives the word; the women who announce the news are a great host."

References for Chapter 5: Heart of the Archer

1. Isaiah 61:1 - "The Spirit of the Lord GOD is upon me, because the LORD has anointed me to bring good news to the poor; he has sent me to bind up the broken-hearted, to proclaim liberty to the captives, and the opening of the prison to those who are bound."

Additional verses:

- Psalm 127:4 - "Like arrows in the hand of a warrior are the children of one's youth."

- Ephesians 6:16 - "In all circumstances take up the shield of faith, with which you can extinguish all the flaming darts of the evil one."

References for Chapter 6: Silent Struggle

1. Isaiah 55:11 - "So shall my word be that goes out from my mouth; it shall not return to me empty, but it shall accomplish that which I purpose, and shall succeed in the thing for which I sent it."

2. Genesis 2:7 - "Then the LORD God formed the man of dust from the ground and breathed into his nostrils the breath of life, and the man became a living creature."

3. Genesis 2:8-9 - "And the LORD God planted a garden in Eden, in the east, and there he put the man whom he had formed. And out of the ground the LORD God made to spring up every tree that is pleasant to the sight and good for food, the tree of life in the midst of the garden, and the tree of the knowledge of good and evil.

4. Ephesians 2:20 - "Built on the foundation of the apostles and prophets, Christ Jesus himself being the cornerstone."

5. John 16:13 - "When the Spirit of truth comes, he will guide you into all the truth, for he will not speak on his own authority, but whatever he hears he will speak, and he will declare to you the things that are to come."

6. Genesis 1:28 - "And God blessed them. And God said to them, 'Be fruitful and multiply and fill the earth and subdue it and have dominion over the fish of the sea and over the birds of the heavens and over every living thing that moves on the earth.'"

7. 2 Timothy 1:7 - "For God gave us a spirit not of fear but of power and love and self-control."

8. Hebrews 8:10 - "For this is the covenant that I will make with the house of Israel after those days, declares the Lord: I will put my laws into their minds and write them on their hearts, and I will be their God, and they shall be my people."

9. Revelation 3:20 - "Behold, I stand at the door and knock. If anyone hears my voice and opens the door, I will come in to him and eat with him, and he with me."

10. 2 Corinthians 3:16 - "But when one turns to the Lord, the veil is removed."

11. 1 Corinthians 2:14 - "The natural person does not accept the things of the Spirit of God, for they are folly to him, and he is not able to understand them because they are spiritually discerned."

12. Hebrews 12:24 - "And to Jesus, the mediator of a new covenant, and to the sprinkled blood that speaks a better word than the blood of Abel."

References for Chapter 7: Out of the Shadowlands

1. James 1:17 - "Every good gift and every perfect gift is from above, coming down from the Father of lights, with whom there is no variation or shadow due to change."
2. Hebrews 12:2 - "Looking to Jesus, the founder and perfecter of our faith, who for the joy that was set before him endured the cross, despising the shame, and is seated at the right hand of the throne of God."
3. John 8:32 - "And you will know the truth, and the truth will set you free." [4] Hebrews 9:14 - "How much more will the blood of Christ, who through the eternal Spirit offered himself without blemish to God, purify our conscience from dead works to serve the living God."
4. Psalm 34:18 - "The Lord is near to the broken-hearted and saves the crushed in spirit."

5. 1 Peter 5:7 - "Casting all your anxieties on him, because he cares for you."
6. Exodus 20:5 - "You shall not bow down to them or serve them, for I the Lord your God am a jealous God, visiting the iniquity of the fathers on the children to the third and the fourth generation of those who hate me."
7. Deuteronomy 7:9 - "Know therefore that the Lord your God is God, the faithful God who keeps covenant and steadfast love with those who love him and keep his commandments, to a thousand generations."
8. Revelation 3:20 - "Behold, I stand at the door and knock. If anyone hears my voice and opens the door, I will come in to him and eat with him, and he with me."
9. John 3:8 - "Whoever makes a practice of sinning is of the devil, for the devil has been sinning from the beginning. The reason the Son of God appeared was to destroy the works of the devil."
10. Isaiah 54:4 - "Fear not, for you will not be ashamed; be not confounded, for you will not be disgraced; for you will forget the shame of your youth, and the reproach of your widowhood you will remember no more. For your Maker is your husband, the Lord of hosts is his name; and the Holy One of Israel is your Redeemer, the God of the whole earth he is called."
11. 1 Samuel 13:13 - "And Samuel said to Saul, 'You have done foolishly. You have not kept the command of the Lord your God, with which he commanded you. For then the Lord would have established your kingdom over Israel forever.'"

References for Chapter 8: Pathways to Freedom

1. Psalm 137:1-4 -"By the rivers of Babylon, we sat and wept when we remembered Zion. There on the poplars, we hung our harps, for

there our captors asked us for songs. Our tormentors demanded songs of joy; they said, 'Sing us one of the songs of Zion!' How can we sing the songs of the Lord while in a foreign land?"

2. Zephaniah 3:17 -"The Lord your God is in your midst, a mighty one who will save; he will rejoice over you with gladness; he will quiet you by his love; he will exult over you with loud singing."

3. James 5:16 - "Therefore, confess your sins to one another and pray for one another, that you may be healed. The prayer of a righteous person has great power as it is working."

References for Chapter 9: Releasing Trauma Prayer

1. Psalm 100:4 - "Enter his gates with thanksgiving and his courts with praise! Give thanks to him; bless his name!" (ESV)

2. Psalm 89:14 - "Righteousness and justice are the foundation of your throne; steadfast love and faithfulness go before you." (ESV)

3. Hebrews 7:25 - "Therefore he is able to save completely those who come to God through him, because he always lives to intercede for them." (ESV)

4. Psalm 136:1 - "Give thanks to the LORD, for he is good. His love endures forever." (ESV)

5. Psalm 36:5 - "Your love, LORD, reaches to the heavens, your faithfulness to the skies." (ESV)

6. Luke 24:32 - "They asked each other, 'Were not our hearts burning within us while he talked with us on the road and opened the Scriptures to us?'" (ESV)

7. John 20:19 - "On the evening of that first day of the week, when the disciples were together, with the doors locked for fear of the Jewish leaders, Jesus came and stood among them and said, 'Peace be with you!'" (ESV)

8. 1 Corinthians 15:6 - "After that, he appeared to more than five hundred of the brothers and sisters at the same time, most of whom are still living, though some have fallen asleep." (ESV)

9. Psalm 91:4 - "He will cover you with his feathers, and under his wings you will find refuge; his faithfulness will be your shield and rampart." (ESV)

10. Jeremiah 29:11 - "For I know the plans I have for you, declares the LORD, plans for welfare and not for evil, to give you a future and a hope." (ESV)

11. Psalm 139:13 - "For you created my inmost being you knit me together in my mother's womb." (ESV)

12. Colossians 2:14 - "Having canceled the charge of our legal indebtedness, which stood against us and condemned us; he has taken it away, nailing it to the cross." (ESV)

13. 1 John 1:9 - "If we confess our sins, he is faithful and just and will forgive us our sins and purify us from all unrighteousness." (ESV)

14. Revelation 12:11 - "They triumphed over him by the blood of the Lamb and by the word of their testimony; they did not love their lives so much as to shrink from death." (ESV)

15. Philippians 4:19 - "And my God will meet all your needs according to the riches of his glory in Christ Jesus." (ESV)

16. Jeremiah 31:3 - "The LORD appeared to us in the past, saying: 'I have loved you with an everlasting love; I have drawn you with unfailing kindness.'" (ESV)

17. Deuteronomy 31:6 - "Be strong and courageous. Do not be afraid or terrified because of them, for the LORD your God goes with you; he will never leave you nor forsake you." (ESV)

18. Zephaniah 3:17 - "The LORD your God is with you, the Mighty Warrior who saves. He will take great delight in you; in his love he will no longer rebuke you but will rejoice over you with singing." (ESV)

19. Thank you to Sandra Sellmer Kersten for sharing her trauma prayer from *Healing Trauma*. https://iapm.live/product-category/books/inner-healing-trauma/

My deepest gratitude goes to Mark Virkler for his unwavering support and guidance throughout this journey. Your wisdom has been a cornerstone in this book.

A heartfelt thank you to Cal Pierce for his constant encouragement and thoughtful insights. Your words have inspired and uplifted me in countless ways.

I am grateful to Sandra Sellmer-Kersten for sharing the powerful *Shame and Trauma* Prayers. Your contributions have brought healing and depth to many..

To Aimee Talbot, thank you for the many nights you spent talking with me, offering your encouragement and support during moments of vulnerability. Your friendship and sisterhood are invaluable, and I am deeply blessed to have you by my side.

A special thank you to my dear friend Deborah Lachance for sitting on the phone with me, patiently reading through every chapter, and reminding me of what I believe and how it ministered to her life. Your insights and encouragement have been a tremendous blessing.

To Jocelyn Drozda, my dedicated editor, thank you for the countless hours you spent teaching me, going through the chapters, and helping me refine my work. Your guidance allowed me to draw inspiration, change the stories, and become more vulnerable in my writing. Your commitment to this project has made all the difference.

Made in the USA
Monee, IL
29 December 2024

75440005R00098